Andrew R. Gottlieb
Editor

On the Meaning of Friendship Between Gay Men

Pre-publication
REVIEWS,
COMMENTARIES,
EVALUATIONS . . .

"One of the most striking things about this collection is the easy integration of personal narrative and cultural analysis. Each of the essays incorporates life stories with acute observations about their meaning within gay male culture and the culture at large. By reading these essays not only can gay men learn more about the value of their own attachments, but also anyone who has valued friendship will find the resources for imagining an infinitely diverse life with others."

Eric O. Clarke, PhD
Associate Professor of English,
University of Pittsburgh

"These essays give voice to the energies that gay men give to friendships, to how instrumental friendships are in the way they come to understand their sexuality and themselves, and how—especially to the most reclusive—friendships become a bridge to a wider world. What surprised me is how deeply AIDS permeates essay after essay and has come to define and transform the meaning of gay friendship. One must go back more than a decade to John Preston and Michael Lowenthal's collection *Friends and Lovers* to find a volume as eloquent about the role of friendship in gay men's lives."

David Bergman, PhD
Professor of English, Towson University;
Author of *The Violet Hour: The Violet Quill*
and *The Making of Gay Culture*

On the Meaning of Friendship Between Gay Men

Titles of Related Interest

Muscle Boys: Gay Gym Culture
By Erick Alvarez

Gay Travels in the Muslim World
Edited by Michael Luongo

When Your Spouse Comes Out: A Straight Mate's Recovery Manual
By Carol Grever and Deborah Bowman

Male Bodies, Women's Souls: Personal Narratives of Thailand's Transgendered Youth
By LeeRay M. Costa and Andrew J. Matzner

On the Meaning
of Friendship
Between Gay Men

Andrew R. Gottlieb
Editor

Routledge
Taylor & Francis Group

NEW YORK AND LONDON

First published 2008
by Routledge
270 Madison Ave, New York, NY 10016

Simultaneously published in the UK
by Routledge
2 Park Square, Milton Park, Abingdon, Oxon OX14 4RN

Routledge is an imprint of the Taylor & Francis Group, an informa business

© 2008 Taylor & Francis

Printed and bound in the United States of America on acid-free paper by
Edwards Brothers, Inc.

Library of Congress Cataloging in Publication Data
  On the meaning of friendship between gay men / [edited by] Andrew
Gottlieb.
     p. cm.
  Includes bibliographical references.
  1. Gay men—Social networks. 2. Gay men—Social conditions. 3. Gay
men—Psychology. 4. Male friendship. I. Gottlieb, Andrew R.
  HQ76.O5 2008
  306.76'62—dc22

                                                              2007045394

Cover design by Jennifer Gaska.

ISBN10: 0-7890-3353-4 (hbk)
ISBN10: 0-7890-3354-2 (pbk)
ISBN10: 0-2038-8944-4 (ebk)

ISBN13: 978-0-7890-3353-6 (hbk)
ISBN13: 978-0-7890-3354-3 (pbk)
ISBN13: 978-0-2038-8944-2 (ebk)

To Ed Musselman
For his twenty-eight years of friendship, and counting.

CONTENTS

About the Editor   xi

Contributors   xiii

Acknowledgments   xix

Introduction   1
      Andrew R. Gottlieb

PART I: TOWARD A DEFINITION OF GAY MALE FRIENDSHIP

1. Why "Friendship" Works—And Doesn't   9
      Frederick S. Roden

PART II: ON FRIENDSHIP AND MENTORSHIP

2. 715 Willey Street   17
      Jeff Mann

3. Time and Tide   31
      Marc E. Vargo

4. The Grounds on Which We Met: Friendship and the Possible   39
      Ed Madden

PART III: ON FRIENDSHIP AND THE GROUP

5. Larry, Me, and "The Family"   47
      Neil Kaminsky

6. Circuitries of Friendship: Camaraderie and Collectivity
      on the Gay Dance Floor   57
      Vincent A. Lankewish

PART IV: ON FRIENDSHIP AND SEXUALITY

7. A Towel and a TV   67
    Michael E. Thomas II

8. More Was Better: Sex with Friends   73
    Chris Packard

9. The Crossing   79
    E. M. Kahn

10. The Country Club   91
    Michael E. Thomas II

PART V: ON FRIENDSHIP AND SPIRITUALITY

11. Soul Friend   99
    Thomas Lawrence Long

PART VI: ON FRIENDSHIP AND BEING ALONE

12. A String Theory of Friendship   105
    Jay Quinn

13. Not Quite There   111
    Felice Picano

14. The Absence: Living Everyday Life Without Gay
    Male Friends   125
    Eric Aoki

PART VII: ON FRIENDSHIP AND SURVIVAL

15. Friends: When Are They Necessary?   137
    Jeffrey Dudgeon

16. Notes from the Apocalypse: A Week with Katrina   143
    Marc E. Vargo

PART VIII: ON FRIENDSHIP AND PARTNERSHIP

17. Subject: friendship   151
    Dan Martin and Michael Biello

ABOUT THE EDITOR

Andrew R. Gottlieb, is a clinical supervisor at the Corona Elmhurst Guidance Center in Jackson Heights, New York and maintains a private psychotherapy practice in downtown Brooklyn. He is also on the editorial board of the *Journal of GLBT Family Studies.* His previous works include *Out of the Twilight: Fathers of Gay Men Speak* (2000), *Sons Talk About Their Gay Fathers: Life Curves* (2003), *Side by Side: On Having a Gay or Lesbian Sibling* (2005), and (with Jerry J. Bigner) *Interventions with Families of Gay, Lesbian, Bisexual, and Transgender People: From the Inside Out* (2006), all Haworth Press books. Visit his Web site at: www.andrewrgottlieb.com.

CONTRIBUTORS

Eric Aoki is an associate professor in the Department of Speech Communication, Colorado State University. He teaches interpersonal and intercultural communication and conducts research in the areas of queer studies, diversity communication, and media and rhetorical studies. As an individual who enjoys teaching and global travel, Eric led a group of university students to Santiago, Chile, in March 2007 for International Alternative Spring Break. He serves on many diversity advocacy committees at CSU, as the Media Reviews Editor for the *Journal of GLBT Family Studies,* and is on the Board of Directors for the Northern Colorado AIDS Project (NCAP) in his local community of Old Town, Fort Collins. During his holiday and summer breaks, he is typically on a plane to journey the globe. Otherwise, Eric can be found oil painting and hosting parties in his painting studio, Studio 23.

Michael Biello and **Dan Martin** have been life partners, creative partners, and friends for over thirty years. As musical theater collaborators, they have written critically acclaimed shows, which have been produced throughout the United States, including their award-winning musical *Breathe* and their new musical-in-progress *The Cousins Grimm.* Their songs have been performed at LaMama, Lincoln Center, on ABC, PBS, and on a variety of recordings. Biello and Martin also operate a studio showroom in Old City Philadelphia where Biello exhibits his illuminated sculptures and Martin composes and produces music. Together they are the cofounders of OUTMUSIC, the international network of LGBT musicians. In December 2004, they were honored with induction into the GLBT Hall of Fame along with the likes of Harvey Fierstein, Billie Jean King, Jerry Herman, Armistead Maupin, Gertrude Stein, and Oscar Wilde. Visit their website at: www.biellomartin.com.

Jeffrey Dudgeon lives in Belfast and was the successful plaintiff at the European Court of Human Rights at Strasbourg in a case against the British government, which led to the decriminalization of male homosexuality in Northern Ireland in 1982. He is the author of *Roger Casement: The Black Diaries—With a Study of his Background, Sexuality, and Irish Political Life.*

After graduating from Bard College in the late 1960s, **Gene Kahn** went into newspaper work back in the days when molded lead type was still used for printing. He calls himself "an old hot type man," to anyone who still knows what that means. Living in the West Village during the heyday of the post-Stonewall era provided Kahn the environment he needed to finally come out. It was during those same free-wheeling, cheap-rent 1970s that he went into woodworking and established a custom shop called Evergreen Studios, Ltd., which produced fancy cabinet work for stores like Laura Ashley and all the Burke & Burke delis around midtown Manhattan. With the recent publication of his memoir, *Deep Water: A Sailor's Passage,* he returns at last to the world of writing. In it, he deals with his many years of sailing, mostly in the Northeast, and chronicles his long-term relationship with Kevin Abend-Olsen, who fell victim to AIDS during the darker years of the epidemic.

Neil Kaminsky is a licensed clinical social worker in California, and author of *When It's Time to Leave Your Lover: A Guide For Gay Men, Affirmative Gay Relationships: Key Steps in Finding a Life Partner,* and *Man Talk: The Gay Couple's Communication Guide.* A native of Brooklyn, New York, he now lives in West Hollywood, California, and is currently working on his first novel.

Vincent A. Lankewish holds degrees in English literature from NYU, Merton College, Oxford, and Rutgers-New Brunswick. He is the author of essays on Victorian and medieval literature, queer theory, and pedagogy and has completed a book manuscript titled *Seeing Through the Marriage Plot: Queer Visionaries in Victorian Literature.* He is at work on a sequel, *Aesthetes in America: A Gay Fantasia on Victorian Themes.* Dr. Lankewish teaches humanities at the Professional Performing Arts School in Manhattan.

Thomas Lawrence Long is professor of English at Thomas Nelson Community College in Hampton, Virginia. He is author of *AIDS and American Apocalypticism: The Cultural Semiotics of an Epidemic* (State University of New York Press, 2005) and editor in chief of *Harrington Gay Men's Literary Quarterly.* He has recently contributed chapters to *Gender and Apocalyptic Desire* (edited by Brenda E. Brasher and Lee Quinby) and *Catholic Figures, Queer Narratives* (edited by Lowell Gallagher, Frederick S. Roden, and Patricia Juliana Smith).

Ed Madden is an associate professor of English at the University of South Carolina, where he teaches creative writing, Irish literature, and gender studies. His poems have been published in many journals and collections, including the anthology *Gents, Bad Boys, and Barbarians: New Gay Male Poetry.* Madden is the poet in residence at the Riverbanks Botanical Gardens in Columbia, South Carolina. His columns and essays have appeared in many newspapers, as well as on National Public Radio's *All Things Considered.* He is one of the founders of *Rainbow Radio,* South Carolina's first gay radio show. In 2006 Madden received a Legacy Award from the Human Rights Campaign of the Carolinas.

Jeff Mann grew up in Covington, Virginia, and Hinton, West Virginia, receiving degrees in English and forestry from West Virginia University. His poetry, fiction, and essays have appeared in many publications, including *The Spoon River Poetry Review, Wild Sweet Notes: Fifty Years of West Virginia Poetry 1950-1999, Prairie Schooner, Shenandoah, Laurel Review, The Gay and Lesbian Review Worldwide, Crab Orchard Review, West Branch, Bloom,* and *Appalachian Heritage.* He has published three award-winning poetry chapbooks, *Bliss, Mountain Fireflies,* and *Flint Shards from Sussex;* two full-length books of poetry, *Bones Washed with Wine* and *On the Tongue;* a collection of personal essays, *Edge;* a novella, *Devoured,* included in *Masters of Midnight: Erotic Tales of the Vampire;* a book of poetry and memoir, *Loving Mountains, Loving Men;* and a volume of short fiction, *A History of Barbed Wire.* He teaches creative writing at Virginia Tech in Blacksburg, Virginia.

Chris Packard grew up in Topeka, Kansas, and now lives and teaches in New York City. A lifelong competitive swimmer, he earned two silvers and one bronze medal at the Gay Games IV in Chicago. He has published short stories and poems in several literary magazines, and collaborated with visual artist Robert Flynt in an exhibition of words and pictures about grief and the AIDS crisis. *Queer Cowboys and Other Homoerotic Friendships in Nineteenth-Century American Literature* (Palgrave, 2006) is his book about how male-male erotic affection undergirds the nation's most popular myths.

Poet, playwright, screenwriter, and essayist, **Felice Picano** is considered one of the founders of modern gay literature. Best known for co-authorship of *The New Joy of Gay Sex* and his award-winning novels *Like People in History, The Book of Lies,* and *Onyx,* he has also written four acclaimed memoirs, most recently *Fred in Love.* His sci-fi masterwork, *Dryland's End,* was reissued in 2004 and his fiction collection, *Tales: From a Distant Planet,* was published in November 2005. A member of the Violet Quill Club, Picano founded and ran the SeaHorse Press and Gay Presses of New York.

Jay Quinn has made his mark on contemporary gay literature with works that deal with issues of family, intimacy, and spirituality, reflecting the lives of men who live outside of a self-imposed ghetto. His most recent novel, *The Good Neighbor,* will be followed by *The Beloved Son,* to be published by Alyson Books in 2007. For five years, he was the executive editor of The Haworth Press Southern Tier Editions and created a list of over sixty titles that brought many new and original voices to the canon. He was also recognized by *OUT* magazine as one of the most intriguing people of 2005. Currently, Quinn makes his home in South Florida with his two dogs and his partner of fourteen years.

Frederick S. Roden is associate professor of English at the University of Connecticut. He is the author of *Same-Sex Desire in Victorian Religious Culture,* the editor of *Palgrave Advances in Oscar Wilde Studies,* and co-editor of *Catholic Figures, Queer Narratives.* His current projects include an edited volume titled *Jewish/Christian/Queer: Crossroads and Identities* and a companion to the works of fourteenth-century mystic Julian of Norwich.

Michael E. Thomas II attended Princeton Theological Seminary after earning a theology/philosophy degree from Geneva College in Pennsylvania. He is president and managing director of The Tomato Group, Inc., which offers training and consulting services. He is a certified trainer for Cornell University's Residential Child Care Project and an independent training consultant and curriculum contributor for the Sanctuary Leadership and Development Institute. Michael has consulted for TD Consultant Group, freelanced for *The Princeton Review,* and recently developed and led a workshop series for LGBT students at the Counseling Center at Lehman College. He has published in the mental health journal *Therapeutic Communities* and recently presented a workshop titled "The Impeccability Factor" at Cornell University's International Residential Care conference in Dublin. In 2004, he cofounded the Make A Stand Project, which promotes success for at-risk young African American men. Michael lives in New York City with his partner, Anthony, and is currently working on a book about creative child care.

Marc E. Vargo is a Psychological Associate IV at the Hammond Developmental Center in Hammond, Louisiana, as well as the author of numerous journal articles in the areas of medical education, neuropsychology, and death anxiety. He is also the author of four nonfiction books, the most recent being *Noble Lives: Biographical Portraits of Three Remarkable Gay Men—Glenway Wescott, Aaron Copland, and Dag Hammarksjöld*. Other titles include *The HIV Test: What You Need to Know to Make an Informed Decision, Acts of Disclosure: The Coming-Out Process of Contemporary Gay Men,* and *Scandal: Infamous Gay Controversies of the Twentieth Century.* Currently, he is at work on a biography of gay mathematician Alan Turing, the wartime cryptanalyst and a pioneer in the field of artificial intelligence. A longtime resident of New Orleans, Marc lives with his life partner, Michael Walker, in the French Quarter.

Acknowledgments

Never in my wildest dreams did I foresee that my first book, *Out of the Twilight: Fathers of Gay Men Speak,* published by The Haworth Press in 2000, would only be the beginning of an exploration of LGBT people and family life that would span the next eight years. While this and the other books that followed were mostly from the perspective of members of our biological families, the present volume is from the perspective of gay men, and is about the creation of our own families of friendship, those "networks of intimacy, affection, and support that resist and exceed the prescribed relationships of family and obligation," in the words of Ed Madden, one of the contributors to this volume.

Needless to say, I could not have done any of this had it not been for all the people at The Haworth Press who have been so good to me. Of particular mention are the two men who initially accepted my proposal, Bill Palmer, the former Publications Director, and John P. De Cecco, Editor in Chief for the Gay and Lesbian Studies book program. I am also indebted to Senior Editor Greg Herren, who gave me an extension on my contract after several prospective contributors unexpectedly dropped out, as well as to Rebecca Browne, Project Manager for the Book Division, who has always been a staunch advocate, not only for me, but for many Haworth authors and editors. Also of mention are those who helped during the production phase, particularly Amy Rentner, Senior Production Editor, and Bill Palmer, my copyeditor.

Of course, this book would not *be* a book without its contributors, who have taken time out of their otherwise busy lives to create original pieces that shed light on that sometimes, difficult-to-define relationship we call friendship. To them, I am and will always be, eternally grateful.

On the Meaning of Friendship Between Gay Men

By helping you, perhaps I was trying to lift up my life a trifle.
Heaven knows anyone's life can stand a little of that.

Charlotte, the spider, to Wilbur, the pig
(Charlotte's Web)

Introduction

Andrew R. Gottlieb

Though born a runt, Wilbur, the central character in the children's classic *Charlotte's Web* (White, 1980), considered himself one lucky pig. Just moments before young Fern's father, John Arable, was ready to get rid of him because he would "never amount to anything" (p. 1), Fern pleaded with him to permit Wilbur to live. Reluctant at first, he finally gave in on one condition: that Fern care for Wilbur. And that she did. Nursing him, feeding him, playing with him, and making Wilbur her very own. So well did Fern do her job that Wilbur grew up quickly, and, in no time at all, was ready to be sold. Although it was hard to give him up, Fern felt better knowing that he was going to live on her Uncle Homer's farm. A loving home for Wilbur was assured.

Quickly, Wilbur met the other animals that lived there: the geese, the sheep, the horses, the cows, the rooster, the gander, the lambs, and, of course, Templeton the rat. Wilbur spent his days eating from the pail of slops, digging holes and trenches, watching the flies, the bees, and the swallows, scratching himself in itchy places, napping, and trying to get acquainted with the other animals in the barn. And even though Fern came to visit him quite often, Wilbur still felt lonely. One day, in the depths of despair, Wilbur heard a new, unfamiliar voice call to him: "Do you want a friend, Wilbur? . . . I'll be a friend to you. I've watched you all day and I like you" (p. 31). Who was that? He couldn't see anyone. He'd have to wait until morning to find out.

Searching high and low the next day, he desperately wanted to know who it was that spoke to him the night before: "Attention, please! . . . Will the party who addressed me at bedtime last night kindly make himself or herself known by giving an appropriate sign or signal" (p. 34)! There was no response. So he repeated himself.

On the Meaning of Friendship Between Gay Men

Still nothing. Then, all of a sudden, a voice: "Salutations" (p. 35)! It was the eight-legged, gray spider Charlotte, formally introducing herself to Wilbur, who had never heard that strange word before. She explained to him how she keeps herself alive on a diet of flies, bugs, grasshoppers, beetles, moths, butterflies, cockroaches, and other assorted insects, trapping them in her web, then killing them and drinking their blood. Fierce, brutal, and scheming, Charlotte had all the qualities that Wilbur didn't like. Could he learn to like Charlotte?

On three big meals a day, Wilbur was getting heavier and heavier. He didn't realize it until the old sheep told him, but Homer was intentionally fattening him up so that he could be sold, then turned "into smoked bacon and ham" (p. 49). Wilbur thought he was hearing things. What was he to do? He wasn't ready to die. He wanted to live and enjoy the company of all his barnyard friends, to smell the clear country air, and to bask in the warm, radiant sunshine. "Who's going to save me," Wilbur cried. "I am" (p. 51), Charlotte said, although how she was going to do it, even *she* didn't know at the time.

Many days were to pass before Charlotte's idea finally came to her. Then, one foggy morning, embedded in her web, Charlotte had written the words: SOME PIG! No one could believe it—not Homer, not his wife Edith, not the farm hand Lurvy. The townsfolk, too, came from miles around to witness this strangest of wonders. Indeed, Wilbur was some pig and Charlotte was some spider who had saved Wilbur's life. It was a miracle.

After a point, Charlotte decided that she and everyone else was tired of reading and rereading the same phrase, SOME PIG. Something new was needed. So after a meeting with the other inhabitants of the barn, it was agreed, at the suggestion of the goose, that the words TERRIFIC PIG would replace it. After living with this for a while, Charlotte then replaced TERRIFIC PIG with the words RADIANT PIG. Wilbur was getting all the attention he could hope for. He glowed—radiantly. How could he ask for a friend better than Charlotte? She had come through for him in a way that he never would have dreamed. For Wilbur, friendship was one of the best, most gratifying things in the whole world.

With summer drawing to a close, everyone was getting revved up for the Country Fair, where Wilbur hoped to further distinguish himself and maybe even win a prize. He wanted Charlotte there beside him, rooting him on. But she wasn't sure if she could go. She was growing old and tired and needed to conserve her energy for her next important job: spinning an egg sac and laying her eggs. But, a true blue friend to the end, Charlotte finally agreed to accompany him and lend support to Wilbur as she always had. Climbing onboard his crate marked ZUKERMAN'S FAMOUS PIG, Charlotte and Wilbur, accompanied by Templeton the rat, were all off to the Fair.

Although he didn't win First Prize, which went to another pig named Uncle, Wilbur did receive a bronze medal and Homer got $25.00. It was a proud moment for all, including Charlotte, who had written yet another accolade, HUMBLE PIG, near Wilbur's crate that day. It was to be her final effort.

During the time at the Fair, Charlotte spun her egg sac, her *magnum opus,* her best, most glorious work: "the finest thing I have ever made" (p. 145), she proclaimed. Inside were 514 baby spiders. Old, weary, and now ready to say farewell to the world, she knew she would not make it back home to the barn. Wilbur was devastated. What would he do without Charlotte? He had an idea: What if he took her egg sac back with him and looked after it until next spring when all the babies would be born? What better way to repay Charlotte, who, after all, had sacrificed so much of herself? So, with the help of Templeton, reluctant though *he* was, the two of them managed to get the sac into Wilbur's crate and take it home with them, ensuring its safety until the day would arrive when all of Charlotte's offspring would be born and eventually make their own marks on the world, just like their mother had.

True to his word, Wilbur did just that, befriending Charlotte's children, grandchildren, and great-grandchildren until the end of his days, just as Charlotte had done so selflessly for him.

Yes, Wilbur was one lucky pig.

It is perhaps inevitable that I've ended up at this place—a book on the meaning of friendship. After so long an exploration of family life, I realized that friendship is perhaps the simplest, least complicated form of family, unencumbered as it is by the myriad of complexities that burden many of our biological families. Friendship is, in the final analysis, a family of choice.

In considering the reasons I wanted to do this volume, it seemed to me that we, as adults, hardly ever talk about friendship and, if we do, it's considered of secondary importance, secondary, that is, to the relationships with our parents, our siblings, our partners, and our children—not the "real stuff" of daily life. Rarely after adolescence, a period in which friendship and the peer group is considered central, do we look at its continuing place in our lives and the multiple meanings it holds.

For gay men, however, friendship has *never* been thought of as secondary. Rather, those relationships have always been safe havens, places where we can be understood, feel valued, and experience acceptance and love. Like Wilbur, born smaller, more fragile, less able to fend for himself—in a word, *different*—whose life takes on meaning only after he finds others, like Fern and Charlotte, who identify with him, see his specialness, rescue him, and forge deep, lifelong connections, we, as gay men, depend on our friends to see something special in us, which then helps us to see that special something in ourselves. Friendship helps us to survive. However, as the contributors in this volume will attest, those relationships can be quite complex.

In Part I: *Toward a Definition of Gay Male Friendship,* Fredrick Roden considers "Why 'Friendship' Works—and Doesn't," expounding on the historical place friendship has held and continues to hold in our queer lives.

Masterfully mixing past and present, metaphor and memory, Jeff Mann opens Part II: *On Friendship and Mentorship,* by taking us to "715 Willey Street," the place where Allen—roommate, artiste, chef, prankster, dance partner, friend—literally and figuratively spins Jeff around, points him in the right direction, and shows us how vital a mentor can be during so critical a stage as late adolescence and beyond. Similarly in "Time and Tide," Marc Vargo fondly recalls Greg, an old-er, out-er gay man, who inhabited Marc's life as Marc inhabited Greg's, each giving to the other just what they needed at an important juncture, propelling them both forward, albeit in opposite directions. "The Grounds on Which We Met" proved fertile ones indeed for Ed Madden, whose first real gay male friend, Ed R., opened his arms and his heart unconditionally, helping Madden to envision another life, one that was not only possible, but inevitable.

At times, friendship not only recreates the experience of what we left behind, it creates something entirely new, as Neil Kaminsky shows us in "Larry, Me, and The Family," the first of two essays that comprise Part III: *On Friendship and the Group,* giving our lives more meaning and depth, but at the same time, leaving us with a heightened sense of vulnerability about the sheer brevity and utter fragility of life. In contrast, Vince Lankewish's "Circuitries of Friendship," is a reflection on his ambivalent relationship with the dance floor and with those on it. A venue first approached with some trepidation, then celebrated, now mourned, it was, nevertheless, one that facilitated a deeper connection to his friends and one that permitted the flame within him to ignite, sparkle, then burn brighter.

Michael E. Thomas II gives us two essays, serving as bookends for Part IV: *On Friendship and Sexuality.* In his first, he discusses how raw, primal, animal lust, as basic as just "A Towel and a TV," cannot only begin a relationship but also set the stage for a deeper connection. He contrasts this with "The Country Club," a piece about how his friendship with Stavito, a friendship infused with sexuality, was perhaps a substitute for and a defense against the fear of a romantic attachment. Sandwiched in between these two pieces is "More Was Better: Sex with Friends," a romp through Chris Packer's adolescence and early manhood, a time when sex was, in a word, *play;* and E. M. Kahn's, "The Crossing," a metaphor for how Kahn gives up the possibility of a sexual connection with Chris, instead offering this smart, confident, adventurous, young man another kind of space in which to explore, another kind of adult relationship in which to grow, with Kahn suddenly finding himself in the new, unfamiliar role of trusted mentor.

In the single essay that comprises Part V: *On Friendship and Spirituality,* Thomas Long pays homage to Ken, his "Soul friend," simultaneously evoking the spirit of medieval Abbott, Aelred of Rievaulx, reminding us of the tradition of soul friendship, one that negates neither body nor spirit, but fully acknowledges and incorporates both.

If we talk about the presence of gay male friendship, then we must also talk about its absence, the subject of Part VI: *On Friendship and Being Alone.* In "A String Theory of Friendship," Jay Quinn offers his own spin on how friendship begins and is sustained. Each of us—tiny, vibrating particles that fill the universe—are sometimes fortunate enough to collide with other, similarly vibrating particles that somehow complement one another, creating a bridge from our own fundamental sense of aloneness and separateness to moments of a shared, harmonious reality. Felice Picano explores his tenuous connection with the detached, enigmatic Bobby Brown, the man-child who is "Not Quite There," the muscle-less, pale, East Texan with the "Dutch-boy" haircut, the world-weary loner, the dreamer, the druggie, who drifted in and out of Picano's life, much like the poltergeist that mysteriously inhabited his Jane Street Greenwich Village apartment he shared for a time with Bobby. In "The Absence," Eric Aoki writes with honesty about the lack of gay male friends in his daily life, exploring the repercussions of living in a smaller, academic community, one in which gay men are practically invisible, the adjustments he has had to make, the ways he feels he can be helpful to others, and his longing for a future that includes other out men, helping him to fill in the crucial missing piece of his life.

Part VII: *On Friendship and Survival* offers two contrasting pieces. In the first, Jeffrey Dudgeon ponders the question: "Friends: When Are They Necessary?" concluding that they *were*, especially during those early days of the gay liberation movement in war-torn Belfast. Less so now, however, in later life, a time when the prospect of making new ones has become more difficult and much less of an imperative. "Notes from the Apocalypse" finds Marc Vargo and his partner Michael Walker in the grips of Hurricane Katrina, fighting for their lives, finally finding refuge and solace from storms—physical and emotional—in the warm embrace of other gay men.

Completing the anthology, Part VIII: *On Friendship and Partnership,* is Dan Martin's and Michael Biello's "Subject: friendship," a simple, quiet, heartfelt e-mail exchange about what their relationship has meant to each of them over the last thirty years, reminding us that friendship is at the core of many long-lasting love affairs.

Toward the end of *Charlotte's Web,* Charlotte acknowledges that it was the act of befriending Wilbur that gave her the chance "to lift up [her] life a trifle" (p. 164)—becoming a way out of her rather humdrum existence and an opportunity to be helpful, giving her life purpose and meaning. In turn, Wilbur expresses his gratitude for all that she has done for him: "I would gladly give my life for you—I really would" (p. 164).

It is my hope that, in reading the essays in this volume, you will reflect upon your own friendships over the years and what those have meant to you. And how, maybe through them, your own life, like Charlotte's, got lifted up "a trifle."

REFERENCE

White, E.B. (1980). *Charlotte's Web*. New York: HarperCollins.

PART I:
TOWARD A DEFINITION
OF GAY MALE FRIENDSHIP

– 1 –

Why "Friendship" Works—
And Doesn't

Frederick S. Roden

Friendship Past and Present

We live at a cultural moment when categories shaping identity—in pairs—are being brought under analysis. For better or worse, that union called "marriage" is subject to interrogation—for same-sex couples as well as heterosexual ones. Some of us who choose to call ourselves LGBT—or queer—love to love, or love to hate, marriage. At the same time, scholarly work on the history of same-sex attachments has tremendous breadth. There are those who would argue that it is impossible to compare a same-sex pair of the twenty-first century to one of the nineteenth. There are also those who see tremendous resonances, so much so that it seems critical to distinguish other variables of identity that separate us from lives experienced at other times and in other places. At this particular moment in LGBTQ history, what

On the Meaning of Friendship Between Gay Men

value does "friendship" have—for ourselves, and as we seek to sculpt and scope a history of sexual diversity? Can friendship be the new marriage and did it serve that role in the past?

By now there is an extensive scholarly history that interrogates the ways that we may find homoerotic desires contained in that category of "friendship." The range of such evidence moves from ancient Greek warriors to medieval knights, from samurai to spinsters. "Romantic" friendship is a term specifically used to analyze those bonds experienced *prior* to marriage, in that liminal space between childhood and adulthood. "Friendship" has been evaluated as a space maintaining same-sex desire for both men and women. Indeed, much of the scholarship locating homoeroticism in friendship comes from feminist history, exploring the lives of unmarried women, in "Boston marriages" or otherwise; or the intimacies of married women whose same-sex attachments offered them something that husbands could not. "Friendship" studies have also been shown to transcend class and race. While the particular manifestations of connections are always shaped by a number of descriptive vectors, "friendship" seems to sustain its value as a vehicle for investigation of hidden homosexuality.

The process of doing this kind of work naturally implies that we are queering, or specifically sexualizing, same-sex friendship. Some scholars argue that all friendships conceal an erotic component, conscious or otherwise. Others are more interested in the ways that such attachments serve as covers for self-aware homosexual subjects seeking an affective home to call their own. Regardless, friendship remains a contested arena for playing out the games of desire—acknowledged or repressed, real or imagined—by scholars attempting to construct a homosexual history.

So where does this critical history leave us, in a historical moment where same-sex desiring individuals inhabit identities that are public rather than covert? If friendship isn't simply a cover, what is its purpose in a post-liberationist, out LGBTQ culture? Where are its affective limits—and differences—with respect to social institutions such as "marriage?" What is a "committed relationship?" Is friendship's commitment the missing link in a manifesto for queer, rather than heteronormative, marriage?

This volume has the distinction of seeking to explore "gay friendship." I can't help but wonder what makes a friendship "gay" and how one gaily lives out a friendship. There's a certain kind of immediate post-Stonewall understanding of "gay friendship" that is really just an extension of all the social historical, feminist explanations of male bonding. Some gay male writers compose odes to friendship that could easily have been produced in times and places much more patriarchal than our own, where men's and women's lives were drastically separate. Does the awareness of homosexual identity magically transform the friendships between gay men into something distinct from male friendship in a patriarchal world? Or is there validity in the (at times homophobic) argument that gay male *communitas* is simply another form of all-male community that excludes women?

The present essay does not seek to extol gay male friendship any more than it looks to indict it. But like "gay marriage," "gay friendship" is a category that can be both dangerously homogeneous and lacking in self-awareness. Is the site of "gay friendship" one that excludes? Is it a space that permits people of the same gender and sexual orientation—and often race and class, to say nothing about political and religious attitudes—to create a safe zone or privileged club? Is "friendship" meant to define a group category or to denote a space of individual intimacy? If we celebrate "gay friendship," are we reinscribing a whole set of qualities that separates rather than welcomes? Does the social unit—whether a "friendship couple" or gay male community of friends—create a discursive space for growth or simply for men's-club ghettoizing?

In suggesting this range of issues, I wish to return to the potential power of friendship, in the way in which it demonstrates, historically and otherwise, how bonds that are not legally sanctioned between people can be individually and collectively empowering. The queer arguments against marriage are dependent on the canonization of unnamed, unsanctified covenants: relationships between individuals who do not necessarily pledge erotic and/or marital-like vows for one another. The extension of rights to people in relationships that *don't* look heteronormative is perhaps the best argument *against* gay marriage as the gold standard for liberation. We have the ability to enfranchise individuals in eldercare pairings, "friendships" (however they might be defined), biological relationships not protected by the law, or non-nuclear families. Within this framework, why not invoke older understandings of the breadth of "friendship" to articulate the law and enlarge our sphere of protection?

The Problem with Friendship

As I suggest above, the best justification for expansion of the category of friendship comes in its form as potential liberational tool concerning same-sex marriage rights rhetoric. Through a reconceptualization of friendship, we have the power to validate—legally and otherwise—a number of kinds of relationships that exist at the margins of a society framed by the nuclear family. However, within a relatively limited understanding of "friendship" there are serious problems. "Gay male friendship" per se has two primary values—one public and one private. In community, wherever two or more are gathered, there is strength: for a voice to speak out against oppression, to support (in a healthy rather than damaging way) self-definition, and thus to serve a marginalized population. Individually, gay male friendship can play a similar function: the communication of self with the other who shares some common category of identity supports the growth and development of the persons involved. The difficulty here is what is shared. To query the process of naming, to what degree do shared sexual orientation and gender identification exist in isolation? That's to say, does "being a gay male" guarantee in and of itself a particular value to the sort of emotional progress described above? On the one hand, is there not a whole nexus of other categories of identity that shape the individual or communal friendship that is being ignored? And might this kind of exclusivity in the development and description of friendship and/or community serve dysfunctions as much as positive results?

On the other hand, how and where do we divide the "nonsexual" gay male friendship from the way in which gay male sexuality is expressed within the relationship or community? There is a continuum here. Desire may be articulated mutually, or shared for some other object. The friendship may even be defined in terms of a "fuck buddy" relationship, a site for sexual relations without marital-like implications. The friendship, or the life in the community, may vacillate between moments of nonerotic attachment and marital-like relationship. But in all of these models, other aspects of what makes up the self come into play. One's age, education, political orientation, ethnic/cultural background, just to name a few, come to shape the dynamics of community and relationship.

What happens when we find unions of desire *outside* of gay male community? Do we call that friendship, and yet a different kind of "friendship" than we privilege *between* gay men? What is the relationship between the canonical *Will and Grace* gay male / straight female pairing and the gay male friendship? In a post-*Queer Eye* age, what of friendships between gay men and "metrosexual" straight men? Given the long history of ambivalence between "separate" gay and lesbian communities, what drives the gay male / lesbian female pairing? In all these other kinds of relationships, there is some element of shared object of erotic desire. Not so in the script for the gay male / lesbian female encounter.

From Innocence to Experience

In Chaucer's *Canterbury Tales,* the Wife of Bath (a disputed object of satire or authorial voice) claims the right to engage the churchmen and practice Biblical hermeneutics on the subject of marriage, right next to ordained theologians. She does so based on "experience": she has lived, has married five times. Alys has the authority to talk about marriage in a way that the priests do not, given their abstract argument. I attempt to have my cake and eat it too (and declare, "let them eat cake!") here. As a scholar who has written on the way that models of friendship have shaped histories of same-sex desire, I nevertheless have obviously lived in friendship. To interrogate the category of the affective cannot occur in isolation; it unfolds in one's own life. What follows is a series of reflections on the academic, the amicitial, and the erotic.

I came of age at a time when out gay identities were visible in the communities I inhabited. Some may have been viewed as being in conflict with other spaces I claimed (the religious, for instance), but they nevertheless were tangible. If my particular proto-gay male childhood meant alliances with the girls in school, adolescence in a single-sex, religiously affiliated prep school didn't offer such options. Hence claiming a kind of queer (but not gay) persona within that space was crucial in a community of compulsory, if repressed and waiting, heterosexuality. I was the eccentric, the aesthete, the intellectual—who got voted best-dressed. My secular college experience that followed failed to realize my dream of coming out to gay male friendships that would ultimately lead to meeting the love of my life. I certainly imagined friendship to exist in such a trajectory toward romantic love. I did awaken to one dream, however. In continuing to cultivate my academic strengths, I found mentors who were eager to support my interest in feminism and gender studies and ultimately to introduce me to the dawn of queer theory.

If individual or group gay male friendship was lacking, I found intellectual *communitas* in books. That experience was hardly different from people of same-sex desire who lived at times and in places where a visible, out and affirming gay subculture didn't exist. I began graduate studies in literature at a private urban university located in a city that boasts one of the largest and most notorious gay populations. Gradually the personal and the professional blended in a variety of ways. I met other gay men; some of them became my friends, some of them I desired. But the only constant was the reality that through my scholarly work I could seek to understand a history (and theology) of people who felt as I did. I became a specialist in religion and homosexuality in literature. In literary studies, I made Oscar Wilde my primary author. But throughout this time, while I had some gay male friends, my deepest friendships were with straight female colleagues. I had no ties whatsoever to the gay community of the city where I studied. I was mentored well by men and women who encouraged my academic work. I delved into scholarly and professional organizations that shared my commitment to the study of same-sex desire in history. The strongest influences on me, that formed my most valued relationships, were people who were queer like me. Few of them were gay men. But all of them transgressed some element of heteronormative identity.

Throughout this time I was reading classically educated writers who dreamed of a romantic ideal. These were the proto-homosexual men whose readings of ancient Greco-Roman literature made them long for a much-awaited idealized friend. My work on such devout Christian men found many who were preparing for the erotic embrace of the Divine Friend alone. It was clear that this model of friendship was firmly shaped within the history of male same-sex desire. Then I met a man considerably my senior. He was brilliant and articulate, and knew this literature and tradition more deeply than I did. He was looking for an ideal. And we fell in love.

This narrative is not meant to canonize that frame as much as to critique it. I have always been old for my years, just as he is forever young. We are many things, but the relationship could never be understood as a classic *erastes/eromenos* model of ancient Greek philosophy, the older lover / beloved youth. Nevertheless, two fantasies and phenomena have consistently shaped our relationship. On the one hand, contrary to a "gay male friendship" imperative that challenges the biological drive, families of origin are central to both of our lives. He showed me photos of his relatives on our first date. Perhaps anyone else would have run away screaming, but I was charmed. We supported one another during his father's death and my great-aunt's decline and eventual death from dementia. She had been one of my queer (if straight) mentors; his mother had died from Alzheimer's disease, so he understood. In short, we both understood each other's concept of community, family, and friendship. Perhaps more understandably, for him an extended community of friends (some gay, most straight) is another family, drawn from an extended period of bachelorhood and a time when many gay male friends had died of AIDS. For me, the only child of an only child, friendship formulates a much smaller, although no less intense, minyan.

For how many couples does friendship create the "basis" of a relationship? However that term gets defined, "friendship" is of course some component of any marital-like relationship. The challenge in heterosexual pairings is how individuals socialized to understand their own gender as potential "friends" and the opposite gender as "the other" can develop romantic relationships based on trust and sharing. In this sense, same-sex relationships have the potential to demonstrate the value of a certain "equal footing" in developing communication among couples.

In both our scholarship and our teaching, my partner and I are strongly committed to work in LGBTQ studies. Yet we do not have visible ties to a gay male community and our friendships tend to take the form of couples (regardless of gender or sexual orientation) or individual relationships grounded in mutual interests or shared beliefs.

Recovering Friendship

In my scholarly writing, I've made the argument that in times and places where homosexuality has been recognized to exist, some same-sex couples have deliberately inhabited and attempted to reinvent or reclaim the category of "romantic friendship." I can't help but wonder at our particular historical moment whether "friendship" might be advantageously reexamined for useful political and social goals.

Perhaps a number of different friendships can exist in the utopia of my imagination. In places where gay male community is necessary for combating social or personal oppression, that *communitas* must be valued and strengthened for its ability to help the individual and group to grow in healthy ways. At the same time, the "gay male friendship" must be interrogated for its dysfunctions. Who is being excluded from gay male community? Who are the outcasts? How can we widen our welcome? For those men who find gay male community and friendship to be essential for self-development and growth, such institutions—at the individual and collective levels—should be supported, provided that they encourage the person to look both within and beyond. Does an individual rely too much on a community (or friendship), particularly one that defines itself by a single aspect of identity? In what ways might that be damaging?

At the same time, I think it is crucial that we explore the means, legally and politically, that family structures differing from marital models can be affirmed. I suggest the category of friendship in exploring these aims because of its breadth. If friendship once articulated a model for alternative family, why not employ such affectional units to legalize and protect these very relationships? Hence rather than family trumping the friendship substitute, we have friendship's non-nuclear models reinventing an extended family. The *communitas* friendship provides may be contained in marital-like pairings, but there are many versions of friendship and caring whose legal recognition and benefit status would protect individuals and families who today are otherwise outside of any definition. If "love is all it takes to be a family," then we need to find ways that "just friends" can no longer be a pejorative category but rather a potential site for the extension of rights to a larger society.

PART II:
ON FRIENDSHIP AND MENTORSHIP

– 2 –

715 Willey Street

Jeff Mann

It betrays my country roots, how awed I am by this sight, a city steaming and gleaming in the rain. Chance or my host's careful choice, I don't know, but this Northern Kentucky hotel room must be the best in the house. It's set high within tonight's storm, overlooking the Ohio River and facing Cincinnati's riverfront, a complexity of bridges, interstates, and glowing office buildings. The scene's dramatic, the view's a privilege. I almost feel as if I've arrived, as if this is some fancy hotel room reserved for rock stars or visiting royalty.

No real star here. I've come to Northern Kentucky University at the kind request of a man who's teaching my new book *Loving Mountains, Loving Men* in his grad class on Appalachian Literature. I've spoken to his students and given a reading. His department has paid for this hotel room. I don't get a lot of these invitations—writing about gay people in Appalachia doesn't net me much money or attention—so it's nice to feel successful for an evening.

As exhilarating as the attention has been, I'm tired after the long day of driving, speaking, and then chatting with folks at the post-

On the Meaning of Friendship Between Gay Men

reading party. I'm glad to be alone now, happy to sit by this big window in the dark and watch the city glitter in the rain. The bed's king-sized—enough room for me and a couple of country-music stars, preferably Tim McGraw and Chris Cagle—but they're inconveniently not here, and I'm too exhausted to do more than cuddle anyway.

Lights in the river: like phosphorescent watercolors, yellow and blue, swirled over a black canvas. Cities: beautiful from a distance, a delight to visit, but I can't imagine living in one. I'm too addicted to solitude and silence, which this hotel room is at present providing. "Chris, Tim, time for bed!" I say, grinning at the foolish impossibility of fancy, heading to the bathroom to brush my teeth. I'm in my late forties: the same decade that has allowed me a small literary reputation has diminished my erotic opportunities and, in consequence, deepened my fantasy life. Thus, these days, Tim and Chris are my houseboys. They don't get much cleaning and cooking done since they spend most of the time shirtless, struggling, sweaty, gagged, and bound back-to-back in my basement. Plus imaginary slaves aren't good dishwashers to begin with.

I'm lying in bed naked, relishing interior fantasy, exterior warmth and quiet, watching the veils of rain diminish, when it hits me.

Cincinnati. Cincinnati.

Last I heard, Allen was living here. Is he still here? Is he even alive? When you don't hear from a college friend for years, if you're a gay man of my generation, you can't help but worry and wonder about the worst.

The phonebook's huge, like most cities'. It takes me a while to find what I'm looking for, but there the name is. He's still on earth. It's not too late, so I call. Machine, not man. But for the first time in fifteen years I hear his voice. I speak into the phone, and somewhere my words are seized by magnetic tape on his answering machine. By this room I will leave tomorrow and never see again, the Ohio River runs by, making small sounds not audible at this distance. Across its rain-stippled black back, restless as history, the city lights spill their aspirations.

Everyone called it Augie's, after the owner. The official name was the Washington Café, at the bottom of Walnut Street, near the Monongahela River. Seedy and friendly, like most gay hang-outs outside large urban areas, with a low bar along one wall, a line of wooden booths along the other. Now it's a small art gallery, but for a few years in the late 1970s it was the only gay bar in Morgantown, West Virginia. It was the first gay bar I ever entered, at age seventeen, the spring of 1977. With only a couple more months of high school to endure before I graduated, I was getting an advance taste of freedom and university life by visiting my lesbian buddy Carolyn, a hometown friend who was attending West Virginia University. She figured it was time for me to glimpse some gay nightlife, so down to Augie's we went. I was excited to be in Queer Space for the first time, and scared too, afraid a horde of homophobes wielding baseball bats might burst in any second. Natural introvert, small-town boy in the city, I sat in a booth with Carolyn, listened to Joni Mitchell on the tiny table jukebox, and watched wide-eyed. I had never seen so many gays and lesbians in one room before.

Carolyn introduced me to several folks that night who would later become enduring friends of mine, and Allen was one of them. The son of a coal-miner, Allen had, like me, grown up in southern West Virginia, in Raleigh County, which adjoins my home county of Summers. He was tall and lean, with short, wavy light brown hair, a handsome, angular face, and large strong hands. It took me only that first evening to discover that he had the kind of quick, mercurial, wicked wit that so many gay men possess, a sharp intelligence I can never match, bulky Caliban that I am, but which I wholeheartedly savor. His whispered comments about this and that bar patron would have done Oscar Wilde proud.

Acerbic he could certainly be, but he was also kind. That evening, he did his best to make me, shy, unsure, shaggy-haired kid that I was, feel at ease. There was, to begin with, no major erotic chemistry between us, which allowed us to skip the complications of sexual attraction and move right into a simpler friendship. Immature men have real problems mixing erotic and platonic love—fucking a friend can ruin the relationship—but we were to be spared those dangers, for the most part.

When, in August 1977, I began my studies at West Virginia University, he and Carolyn were sharing an apartment in a broken-down old house in Sunnyside, Morgantown's student ghetto. I was living in Boreman Hall, an old brick dorm on the Downtown Campus, with a clod-like roommate from Greenbrier County who decorated the walls with *Penthouse* pin-ups and did laundry at two in the morning. I've never been particularly patient, I've always cherished privacy, not to mention uninterrupted sleep, and, besides, I'd come to college not only to get an education, but to spend time with other queers, so it wasn't long before I was sleeping most nights on the lumpy couch in Allen and Carolyn's University Avenue apartment. (*How did I stand it?* I wincingly ask myself at age forty-seven. The answer: an eighteen-year-old back.)

Carolyn I'd gone to high school with. Allen I had only begun to know. Nevertheless, he never complained about my regular presence in their apartment. On the contrary. In I'd stump, rain beading on my leather jacket and in my sparse beard, and there he'd be, smoking and studying by the window or hunched over his sketchpad creating another amazing image with ink or watercolor. Far more cognizant of the gay world than I—in fact, more competent and knowledgeable in just about everything—Allen took me under his wing. He told me about gay bar etiquette, the fine points of cruising, the ins and outs of oral and anal sex. I hardly knew how to make instant coffee—I'd been spoiled by the good cooks in my family but had as yet learned none of their skills—but Allen was an old hand in the kitchen. He cooked us stews, baked macaroni and cheese, on snowy nights whipped up the Unofficial West Virginia State Dish—brown beans and cornbread. We played Joni Mitchell, Janis Ian, and David Bowie into the wee hours, sitting at the little kitchen table studying side by side: his Sociology and Costume Design, my British Lit and Aesthetics. With Carolyn, Laura, Cin, and other lesbian friends, we'd bustle into the Fox—the latest gay watering hole now that Augie had died and the Washington Café had closed—where Allen would advise me on alcohol options like Tequila Sunrises and Harvey Wallbangers (a far cry from the neat Scotch I favor today) and coach my uncoordinated body in the various bump-and-grind dance moves appropriate to the thumping music of Donna Summer and the Village People. I had never danced with a man before, but Allen was a patient teacher.

We had our hard times. From this distance, both the pleasures and the adversities of college days seem unnaturally vivid, as if I stand in the gentle hills of the Piedmont looking back on a sheer mountain landscape I've recently passed through successfully but with some effort, a world far more dramatic and more difficult to traverse than the one I inhabit now. One night we returned to Allen's apartment to discover that someone had broken in and taken the few things of value. Another time, an anonymous someone called to mutter homophobic threats. Once, during that savage winter of 1977-1978, when snow layered the ground in November and stubbornly remained, with regular supplements from the sky, till March, when I was constantly being hailed by complete strangers to help them push their wheel-churning cars out of drifts, the heat in Allen's apartment failed for forty-eight hours and we ended up sleeping together in a completely unerotic attempt to avoid freezing to death. At the end of my first semester, Carolyn quit school and moved out; a charmer named Larry moved in, stayed a few months, then decamped to Florida with Allen's best blazer, leaving behind an enormous long-distance phone bill Allen ended up having to pay. I developed a huge infatuation for one of Allen's friends, Bob, a handsome and thoroughly superficial Italian-American guy from Weston, was far too shy to make my interest known, and then one night lay in agony on the couch listening to Allen and Bob make drunken, noisy love in the adjoining bedroom. I didn't speak to Allen for a few weeks after that.

Despite minor conflicts, we decided to become roommates, for I was hot to escape dorm life. By the beginning of my sophomore year, Allen and I were sharing the second-floor apartment at 715 Willey Street. That address now, as resonant for me as Proust's madeleine, evokes futile nostalgia, a clichéd longing for the Lost Abode of Youth in which those inescapably middle-aged tend to indulge. During my brief returns to Morgantown, I sometimes drive past that house, and its present decrepitude reminds me both of the relative rapidity with which all I know and love is gradually leaving this earth and of that circle of friends—Allen, Laura, Cin, Kaye—who helped me survive my youthful despair, sexual frustration, and loneliness.

Odd what returns to me, almost thirty years later, poised here over my keyboard. I live in Virginia now, with John, my partner of ten years, in Pulaski, a small mountain town very much like the ones I grew up in. I'm publishing books, teaching university students. My beard and chest hair are full of gray, and just lately I have started to notice that same silvery glitter in the fur on my forearms. I have several gay acquaintances, not one truly close gay male friend. I haven't seen Allen in almost twenty years. Still, typing this, I find my way back.

Allen is preparing Cornish game hens, the first I've had. But before they're baked, the hens must dance. Allen's whimsical humor so often pulls me from my depressions. One minute I'm lying in front of our gas fireplace brooding over my celibacy and the cursed and unerring accuracy with which I desire men who have no desire for me, and the next, at Allen's suggestion, we are dangling the hens by their little wings and propelling them in a complex pas de deux across the kitchen table. They bow, they leap, they circle like passionate partners, the Ballet of the Dwarf-Fowl. Allen and I laugh till we hurt.

I'm sitting at the kitchen table making index cards to help me memorize dendrology facts more efficiently—maples have opposite leaves, black walnut leaf scars look like clown faces—when Allen, in one of his frequent prankish moods, slips up behind me. He gently hooks my nostrils with two fingers, pulls my face up and back while I grin and cuss, admires the piggy-nose configuration he's created, says "Oink, Oink, Pussy-Face!" then lets loose and bounds beyond the reach of my play-punch. Ever since my beard has started to fill in, he calls me Pussy Face. He also has elaborate jokes about how much I supposedly love to rim German Shepherds. We're boys from small towns in southern West Virginia: rank humor is par for the course.

"Oh Gawd, it's the Dana and Kaye Show!" I whisper, sticking my head into Allen's overheated bedroom. He's always turning the little heater in his room up and then sleeping under nothing but a sheet, even in the bitter winter weather. I drag him into my bedroom, where the window's cracked a bit even in January and quilts are heaped in layers upon the rarely washed sheets. "Now listen!" I urge, handing him the glass. He puts it to the bare wood floor, listens a minute, and grins. Even without the aid of the glass, I can make out "Oh . . . my . . .

*God . . . Dana!" Lesbian love-making at its loudest. "We should in-
vite folks in and charge for this!" I say, eager entrepreneur.*

*Allen's driving us back from Frostburg, Maryland, where we've
dropped off Lisa, a lesbian friend. While there, Lisa's cronies coaxed
me into trying my first bong. Pot is something I've smoked socially,
but it's never really hit me before. Now, sitting in the passenger seat
and watching the purple-gray mountains stream by, I'm so fucking
high I hardly know where I am. It's scary as hell, though I try to act
calm, fight back the panic, and just listen to the tape Allen's got playing. It's at this point in my chemical confusion that a helicopter appears in silhouette against the sunset's red West.* Lord God, I think,
am I hallucinating? Was there angel dust in that weed? Is my mind
screwed up for good? *As casually as I can, I say, "Uh, man, look at
that. Uh, what, uh . . .?" I'm afraid to say "Look, is that a helicopter?" because I'm half-convinced that he isn't seeing what I'm seeing, which would mean that my brain is ruined and I'll be trapped in
Semi-Rutabagahood for the rest of my life. Allen says, "That's a
sweet chariot come for to carry you home, you hopped-up
cocksucker!" I choke, he laughs and pats my thigh. "Take a nap,
Jeff," he says, and I do.*

*It's a windy April evening. We've been listening to the house creak,
sprawling on the floor in front of the gas fire, indulging in what is very
expensive beer to students as poor as we are, the rare elixir Michelob
(which, in my much later beer-snob days, I'll describe as a product
that "ain't fit to douche a dog"). We're telling ghost stories—I have
the drowned lady who haunts Bluestone Reservoir, he's got some kind
of mine-disaster specter. "Well, I'm hitting the sack," says Allen, just
about the time I'm thoroughly creeped out. "Sweet dreams," he says
wickedly, closing his bedroom door. Trying to relax, I piddle around
ineptly on my new guitar—Joni Mitchell's exotic tunings are challenging for a novice—then head for bed myself.*

*Shucking off my clothes, I slip between grimy sheets. I lie there in
the dark, thinking about mine ghosts and monsters. The wind rattling
the window screen right beside my bed isn't helping, so I grab a*

Kleenex, close my eyes, and start constructing a detailed fantasy about the beefy black-bearded boy I heartily and hopelessly covet in dendrology class. I've got a rag tied between the stud's teeth, his hands roped behind his back, and am lapping his hairy beer belly when something scratches the screen. I start, drop my dick, stare into the darkness. The scratching continues—I'm seeing four-inch-long claws—then a sinister something rasps, "Jeffffff . . . ." Suddenly the screen rattles and a white face is pressed against the window.

"Holy Fuck!!" I shout, leaping out of bed with a rapidly declining hard-on just about the time laughter starts rolling through the screen. It's that bastard Allen. He's climbed out of his bedroom window onto the top of the porch roof and crawled over to my window, all to see if he can make me piss myself. By the time he climbs back in, I'm poised to tackle him. We roll around for a while, laughing and cussing, before he pins me down. I'm the bearded, butch, aspiring leatherman, but he's always the one who wins our wrestling matches. He's always been stronger.

Allen graduated at the end of that year. We parted uneasily. I was selfish and dominating, he was tired of catering to me, he said. I found other accommodations, with a rule-bound recluse I took to calling the Sterile Cuckoo. After a few months of his obsessive-compulsive behavior, I moved into a shabby two-room place on Falling Run Road and began what was to be a long series of years living alone. Mutual friends informed me that Allen's social work degree wasn't of much use in the work world, and pretty soon I heard that he was living with his Aunt Lil near Beckley and working in a tollbooth on the West Virginia Turnpike.

We reestablished contact fast—rural Appalachia is a fairly hostile environment, so gay boys there need to stick together. Soon, during my summers home in Hinton, I would spend a weekend every now and then in Stanaford, the Beckley suburb where he'd grown up and where his parents and aunt still lived. Allen and I would drive an hour down the West Virginia Turnpike to Charleston, the state capital, and the Grand Palace, a gay bar of many years' duration, to gyrate on the checkerboard of the dance floor, an elevated structure lit from within, to drink cheap beer, and to watch the big-haired drag queens cavort.

As usual, Allen flirted with ease, while I avoided the guys I found attractive, far too insecure to introduce myself, much less ask them to dance. Allen, bless him, saved every other dance for me.

Worn out with hours of disco, we'd face a 2 a.m. drive through the dark mountains of Kanawha, Fayette, and Raleigh Counties back to Stanaford. (We gay folks in rural regions will drive a long way for some precious time with Our Own Kind.) We'd sleep together—only once did cuddling lead to more, a quiet coupling with his aunt snoring in the next room, a little 69ing that left minimal morning-after awkwardness and was never spoken of afterwards. Put two young and perpetually horny gay men in a bed, and something's bound to happen sooner or later. From the perspective of middle age, I would say that's reason not for judgment but for celebration. Even in my twenties, the concept of *carpe diem* made perfect sense to me.

Then those late-morning breakfasts courtesy of Mizz Lil, biscuits with sausage gravy made not from milk but water, along with eggs, juice, and lots and lots of coffee. Most folks from my neck of the woods, however modest their means, are superbly hospitable, and I soon learned where Allen had inherited his culinary skills. Nights we didn't drive to Charleston would be composed of stiff drinks and big meals, TV and gossip. Breathless as a Tennessee Williams heroine, Lil would tell tale after tale. Once she gasped, "I took my prescription to the drugstore, and, Lord God, it cost me fifty dollars for four pills. 'Fifty dollars for four pills!?' I said, 'I swan, I'm going to the liquor store, I'm going to buy a bottle of rum, I'm going to go home and have a rum and coke, I'm going to have a rum and coke if it hairlips the president!' I did, I said, 'Fifty dollars for four pills . . . I'm going to have me a rum and coke and I don't care if it hairlips the president!' Indeed I did, I said . . . " When, years later, I read Florence King's *Confessions of a Failed Southern Lady* in which she claims that many Southern women feel compelled to say things three times, I could only grin at the familiar rhetorical pattern.

How did Allen and I drift apart? I finished undergraduate school, then graduate school, lived in Washington DC for a bleak and lonely semester, returned to West Virginia, and began teaching as an overworked and poorly paid instructor in the English Department at WVU. Allen saved his turnpike money and then returned to WVU for a degree in art. He settled down with a new lover, McCarty, in a Tudor-style house not far from my apartment. There we were in Morgantown again, but both so busy there was little time together. He took me down into the bowels of the maze-like Creative Arts Center a few times to show me his sculpture studio, and I attended his senior exhibit. After years of painting, he was focusing on sculptures now, creating disturbing constructs that often evoked the AIDS crisis—slate-gray boxes with shards of mirror and dangling bones. One he gave me, and it stood ominously in my living room until I moved to Blacksburg in 1989. It was too large to take with me; I gave it to McCarty. Their relationship had apparently been provisional from the first—Allen knew he'd be leaving, going to grad school—so McCarty was left with an apartment full of Allen's paintings and sculptures, while Allen moved on to Cincinnati about the time I got a new job at Virginia Tech.

How did we lose touch so completely? Both of us had new lives, in towns far apart. Neither was good at steady correspondence. I made a new set of friends in Blacksburg, fell wildly in love with a man already partnered, grieved terribly when he and his lover left town, then, desperate for consolation, slept around as much as possible. Eventually I met John, my present partner. Eventually I got a postcard announcing an art show of Allen's in Cincinnati. In 1998, I sent him a copy of *Bliss,* my first poetry chapbook, but heard nothing back. Allen had always been the kind of independent friend who waited for invitations from others to jaunt out together but rarely initiated contact himself. I'm the proud sort who thinks, "Now it's *your* turn to get hold of *me.*" I construct little tests for people, count things up, brood over tit for tat. Bad combination. "Well, fuck this," I thought, hoping for and never receiving a note from him gushing over the quality of my poetry. Laura and Kaye, when I saw them during vacation visits, always asked me about him but had never heard from him either. He'd moved to Ohio and simply vanished. "Well, that's what comes from living in the Midwest," I growled, more devoted to my mountains than ever.

Why have I had so few gay male friendships? I wonder this a lot in my middle years. I've had many good lesbian friends, quite a few good straight friends, but almost no close gay friends. There was James, someone I met through Larry, the handsome liar who'd left Allen with that unpaid phone bill so long ago. James and I had an on-again/off-again friendship for two decades. I envied him his string of desirable butch-bottom lovers, and he relished my envy, as well as the way my solitary charmlessness, like leaden foil, accentuated his gemlike charisma. Fallings out, years without contact, reconciliations . . . until, in Rehoboth Beach in the late 1990s, over the pettiest of reasons, one estrangement finally took. More recently, there was David, who kept his careful distance at the same time that he relished my cocktails and I relished his eminently quotable wit. He left town recently, and he was palpably chilly to me at our last meeting, for reasons I have yet to discern. My only present gay male friends are Dan and Phil, though the relationship is long-distance now that John and I have moved to Pulaski. We share weekends of martinis and Manhattans, comfort food, and Netflix two or three times a year.

Am I too rural in my values to appreciate or be appreciated by most other gay men, who are largely urban and urbane? Am I too somber, the dark poet who stands in the corner brooding amidst the glittering party chatter? Too self-consciously butch, the token leatherbear, the bearded BDSM guy who makes the vanilla types nervous? I don't want to talk about home appliances, the Tony Awards, Project Runway. I want to talk about mythology, country music, poetry, guitars, and pickup trucks.

Ah, too late to change. This ole dawg needs no new tricks. I have John, I have family, I have my work, I have sufficient friends old and new. Still, I look backwards as often as I look forward, for the years behind begin to outnumber the years likely to come. I want those friends of my youth to know how much their help meant at that crucial point in my development. I want, if possible, to see them all again, faces creased by the same decades that have creased mine. Thus, after years without contact, that phone call I made from a Northern Kentucky hotel room, overlooking the subtle and ceaseless black flow of the Ohio.

Here's that phone call's answer, one evening a month later, here in Pulaski, with Holly, our one local queer friend, over for dinner. I'm warm on Irish whiskey, we're all three full from another of my big, fattening country meals, relaxing in the living room, watching the cats chase one another, when the phone rings. It's Allen. He's using the phone number I left on his answering machine. Amazed, I carry the phone into the dark library and sprawl on the couch for a good twenty minutes, laughing, catching up, reminiscing, before John appears at the door, annoyed, pointing out what a bad host I'm being. "It's Allen, dammit!"—I'm a specialist in the subtle snarl—"You've heard me talk about Allen. I haven't seen him in fifteen years!" John cocks an eyebrow—he's a specialist at tacit disapproval—and returns to keep Holly company.

I'm too Southern not to get off the phone fast—bad manners are indeed the ultimate accusation—but I've heard what I need to know. Allen's still sculpting in Cincinnati, piecing together a living at this and that (as artists often must), as healthy and vigorous and witty as ever. We agree that it's been too long, that we must set up a meeting soon. What's unspoken is that we're both approaching fifty. The time that might allow for reunions is dwindling fast.

An interviewer once asked me what I missed most from my gay youth, and I replied, with only a little hesitation, "Dancing." I left behind my dancing days in 1989, when I moved from Morgantown, with its conveniently located downtown gay bar, to Blacksburg, where the nearest gay bar is in Roanoke, a forty-five-minute drive away. Living now in Pulaski, I only get to gay bars when John and I travel, to DC, San Francisco, New Orleans, and those bars are almost always bear or leather bars, where there's little to no dancing. I guess it's thought not butch enough.

I have a trifling secret. My partner doesn't know this yet, but I'll share it with you. When I lift weights in our basement—the Radon Gym, I call it, since the radon test results were declared "inconclusive"—in between sets, I shadowbox and dance. I always play loud music when I lift, usually Melissa Etheridge, and most songs have sufficient beat for me to move to. There I am, a beefy, silver-bearded, bald leatherbear in wife-beater, camo shorts, and weightlifting gloves, an overgrown boy with pumped-up hairy chest, tattooed arms, and a sheepish grin. I twitch my hips, hump the darkness, and punch the air, my only partner/rival/lover the wide-shouldered shadow moving along the wall. The few boxing moves I learned a year or so back at the Virginia Tech Boxing Club, the few dance moves are those same ones Allen taught me long years ago, when I was so young, so ignorant, so innocent, and so in need of the guidance he gave me. I never could master the complex disco steps at which Allen was so adept. He was always the better dancer.

Time and Tide

Marc E. Vargo

It was a cold, gray winter in San Francisco. The year was 1980 and I was spending Christmas house-sitting at a friend's apartment in the city. Wrapped in a quilt, I was copyediting manuscripts for the Journal of Rural Community Psychology while waiting for the spring semester of graduate school to begin. Granted, this was not an exciting way for a young gay man to spend the holidays, but this was where fate seemed to have dropped me and I accepted it without protest. As for my friend Greg, the urbane man in whose apartment I was now staying, he was two thousand miles away on the sun-splashed beaches of Acapulco enjoying a sex holiday. Such were the disparities between our lives.

I began writing the above essay at the request of a more recent friend, Andrew Gottlieb. I thought it would be a fairly straightforward task, since everyone knows the definition of friendship: the state of goodwill that exists between two people who share a knowledge of one another, along with mutual trust and affection. I assumed that I would merely need to apply this definition to those of us who enjoy an affinity for our own gender, specifically to Greg and me, and that the piece would naturally unfold. Yet as it happened, I discovered that the task was not really so simple. The more I thought about it, the more I recognized that "gay male friendship" could be understood in many ways and along different dimensions; that it was far more complex than I had originally believed. I therefore decided to set aside for a moment my account of my relationship with Greg so that I might ponder, more deeply, the meaning of this form of friendship.

On the Meaning of Friendship Between Gay Men

I realized, first of all, that anytime two gay men are friends, their relationship fits the definition of a gay male friendship in a strictly technical sense. This is rather obvious. But I also realized that simply sharing a sexual orientation in and of itself does not necessarily add a great deal to a relationship. In my own life, I have had friendships with heterosexual men and women in which I experienced more love, kindness, acceptance, and permanence than I found in some of those I had with other gay people. Merely possessing a similar sexual orientation, then, does not automatically confer upon a friendship a unique element or render it inherently superior. It would be akin to talking about "tall male" friendship: simply because two men are tall does not mean that height necessarily plays a critical role in their relationship or causes it to surpass all others.

At the other end of the spectrum, and more in line with my bond with Greg, is that form of gay male friendship in which the men's sexuality is indeed a central element, one that imbues the relationship with a distinct meaning. The fact that the two men share a sexual orientation, particularly an orientation that does not conform to society's norms, sets the relationship apart from other ones in their lives. In such an alliance, the sense of commonality, of speaking the same language, and of living through comparable experiences in the emotional, sexual, social, and political realms, may both define and sustain the friendship. It may even be its *raison d'etre*. In my own gay relationships of this sort, I've enjoyed profound emotional support, understanding, and encouragement, with such friendships serving as safe havens during times of trial and as clarifying lenses during moments of confusion and indecision. My conclusion, then, is more or less self-evident: friendships between gay men exist on a continuum ranging from those in which sexual orientation is irrelevant to those in which it is truly paramount. And this brings me back to Greg, since our relationship belonged to the latter class.

We first met in Fresno in the autumn of 1979. An Illinois native, I had just completed a masters degree in clinical psychology and moved to this city in the San Joaquin Valley to begin advanced studies at the California School of Professional Psychology (CSPP). Like countless men and women before me, I had also come to the coast to explore life beyond the Midwest. As for CSPP, it was a private graduate school founded by the California Psychological Association and offered doctoral-level training in clinical psychology. Although the school was not particularly pricey at the time, the tuition strained my budget all the same, with matters becoming even worse as tuition increased each year that I attended. Before long, I realized that, from a purely financial standpoint, I had probably chosen unwisely.

Greg, on the other hand, never wanted for cash. Five years older than me, he had a masters degree from San Francisco State and drove a jet-black Cadillac at a time when Cadillacs were still considered cool. The first time I saw him, we were registering for classes and he struck me as different—and in a refreshing way. Tan, nonchalant, and unruffled to the point of laxity, he eyed me from afar, sizing me up, a knowing smile playing across his face. Evidently, I passed his test because he approached me, introduced himself, then under his breath began making wry comments about the other students standing around us, many of whom appeared to be moneyed members of the Palm Springs set. What Greg was doing, of course, was putting me at ease—leveling the playing field, as it were—and I was touched by his humanity.

At the same time, however, I also wondered if this new person in my life, this man who clearly wished to be my friend, felt he was performing some sort of *noblesse oblige,* that of taking a Middle American rustic under his wing. This prospect bothered me for weeks, since I wasn't really provincial and didn't want to be perceived as such. As a child and adolescent, I had spent my days in training as a classical musician, even working briefly at one point with renowned Czech composer and conductor Vaclav Nelhybel, the former musical director of Radio Free Europe. A few years later, as a college student, I set out to further expand myself by traveling to the North African nation of Morocco as part of an exchange program, a small adventure during which I studied cross-cultural psychology while also enjoying flings with both women and men. So no, I did not think of myself as callow nor did I want others to see me in that way. Still, it is evident to me now that my experiences up to that point had been rather narrow, that while I had managed to acquire a respectable knowledge of the arts and sciences, I was behind the curve in other respects, most notably in financial matters (hence my choice of a doctoral program I could ill afford) and in certain sexual areas.

The fact is, I thought that I was bisexual at the time, a mistaken assumption that amazes me to this day. I truly did not understand what it meant to be a gay man, since I had known so few of them, at least those who were forthright about it. And this is where Greg's entrance into my life proved to be so enlightening and so consequential. Not only was he the most openly gay man I had ever met, but he also recognized my own sexual confusion—instantly upon meeting me, it seems—and decided to help me better understand myself. Much later, he even admitted this to me.

And this, I have observed, is a common state of affairs in certain gay male friendships: one of the partners is better informed about what it means to be gay than the other one. The more knowledgeable partner may also be more sensitive to the full measure of the other's homosexuality, more able to detect in the friend what the friend cannot wholly recognize in himself. And the result is both predictable and commendable. The "veteran" may feel duty-bound to help "bring out" his friend, familiarizing him with the meaning of a gay identity, acquainting him with the gay subculture, fostering his self-acceptance, and encouraging responsible sexual experimentation.

With Greg and me, this facilitative process was present from the beginning. When we initially met, Greg said he was from New Orleans and had moved to the West Coast to establish an investment firm. A few weeks later, after he had come to trust me, he confessed that he had actually moved to San Francisco with little money but with a big interest in gay life. Shortly after arriving—and solely out of curiosity—he performed in a gay sex film, then with a business partner invested his limited funds in what quickly proved to be a lucrative sex club in the city's South of Market district, ground-zero at the time for leather bars and bathhouses. When I asked him the name of it, he said, as if it should be obvious, "The South of Market Club," and invited me to visit it. I hesitated, of course, not sure of what I might be getting myself into, so Greg set about describing it to me. He explained that it was quite large, was popular in the Bay Area, and was well-known for its gloryholes. Not surprisingly given my background, I had no idea what a gloryhole was, but I thought it sounded vaguely patriotic. (Maybe I was a rube, after all.) As it happened, I never became a member of his club, although I did agree to keep his ownership of it under wraps, concerned as he was that it might damage his reputation with the other students in our school.

As to why Greg was in a graduate program in psychology in the first place, he said he had tired of the sex scene in San Francisco and wanted to focus his life on something more significant. He also wished to help gay men who were having difficulty coping and believed that becoming a therapist would be an ideal way to do it. In a sense, then, the two of us had met at a moment when we were seeking to move into each other's sphere. That is to say, Greg wanted to become more centered and studious while I wished to become more experimental and expansive. Our friendship thus allowed us to facilitate one another's growth in largely opposite directions.

It was at this time, for instance, that I received an education in all things gay, thanks in no small measure to Greg. He took it upon himself to acquaint me with everything from Harvey Milk's politics to a large circle of gay men in an assortment of professions. The latter proved especially beneficial, since they not only helped me recognize that my previous assumptions about gay people had been off-base, but also allowed me to realize that, like them, I was "exclusively homosexual" in the parlance of the times. And this was fine with me; I was glad to finally have some clarification on the matter. Moreover, now that I had a better understanding of myself and possessed a healthy dose of self-respect, I felt confident enough to enjoy a serious romance with another man.

His name was Ben, and I ran into him in a library in Berkeley. A good-looking Jewish guy from the East Coast, he had dark curly hair, blue eyes, and a warm smile. We met in the stacks, but ended up in his apartment by the end of the afternoon. This was not the end of it, however. We remained together for a year, until it came time for me to leave California for a psychology internship at LSU Medical School in New Orleans.

From my first encounter with Ben until our inevitable goodbyes, Greg stood by me, supportive from start to finish, even though he once hugged me and said with a grin, "You know I'm jealous, don't you?" He also tutored me in the etiquette of gay dating and occasionally gave me relationship advice. In return, I helped him develop effective study habits—*lesson number one, put away the vodka*—critiqued his writing, and offered him pointers on diplomacy within the profession, tactfulness not being Greg's forte at the time. By the end of my stay in California, he was spending his nights at his apartment in San Francisco buried in texts on Jungian psychology while I was at home in the Valley making love to Ben. We were each where he wanted to be, and it was good.

As I reflect on this period in our friendship, I find myself appreciating its resiliency. It seems to me that a true friendship is akin to a living organism in that it must be allowed to breathe and stretch and grow. For a gay male friendship, such flexibility is particularly important, since certain events that are unique to gay men may arise and place a strain on the relationship. Of these, perhaps the most challenging is the entrance of another man into one of the friends' lives, a love interest to be precise. In our case, Greg not only accepted my love for Ben without dwelling on whether it might compete with our friendship, but he actually encouraged the romance. As a result, I found that my bond with Greg deepened. Alas, it outlived my intimacy with Ben to become one of the most enduring relationships of my adult life, if only in memory. This was because Greg died shortly after I left California.

I was living in his hometown, New Orleans, when it happened, having finished my internship and taken a job in the neurology department at the same medical school. I had known for several weeks that Greg had been ill and that he planned to come back to New Orleans, presumably to live out his final days. I was waiting for him to return so we could be together again, but unfortunately he didn't make it back in time. Upon his demise, our school awarded him a posthumous doctoral degree and asked that I make a statement at his funeral.

As for Greg's illness, it was said to have been cancer, although a friend in San Francisco phoned to tell me—to warn me, really—that it was due to a new and lethal gay-related disease. The syndrome was so recent that the term AIDS had not yet been coined; Greg's case was among the first in the nation. I was also told that I could expect to be interviewed by the Centers for Disease Control, since the organization was trying to determine if the condition was infectious and, if so, the means by which it was spread. Although Greg and I had not been sexually intimate, we had been in close proximity for quite some time and therefore a concern existed, unfounded as it turned out, that this nearness may have placed me in jeopardy. I lived with an immense fear of AIDS for the next few years, until researchers finally established its mode of transmission.

As could be expected, I was profoundly hurt by Greg's death, but this loss gradually led to my determination to act. More to the point, the senselessness of his premature passing produced in me a resolve to help other gay men who were confronting AIDS. Since I was working in a medical school at the time, I was fortunate that I had easy access to the research findings that soon began flooding the literature. I also joined an AIDS service organization in New Orleans, the NO/AIDS Task Force, and for the next thirteen years counseled gay men who were undergoing testing for antibodies to the virus. Most significantly, in 1992 I published my first book, which dealt with the subject of AIDS and was dedicated to Greg. Like his life, Greg's death had been instructive to me, prompting me to exercise caution in my love life, while also spurring me to help those at risk for the infection.

It has now been twenty-five years since I met him, yet Greg remains with me in spirit. I also believe that we succeeded in influencing one another's lives and entering into each other's realm.

A couple of years ago, I had just released another book, this one having to do with gay legal controversies, when the editor of the Australian magazine *Blue* contacted me. For those who are unfamiliar with it, *Blue* is an upscale coffee-table magazine that features articles about men in the arts and includes high-toned photos of nude men. The editor explained that the magazine planned to run a story about my new book and asked if I would consent to an interview. I agreed, of course, and found it to be a pleasant experience. I was also pleased with the article that resulted, a finely crafted piece by Sydney journalist Tim Benzie. What most caught my eye, however, were the magazine's stunning photos of men in their natural states. These included a remarkable series of images by Greek photographer Dimitris Yeros that featured sleek Mediterranean men, as well as a collection by French photographer Jean Quelquejeu which consisted of close-ups of bronze adonises. Breathtaking, too, was a compilation by New York fashion photographer Michael Reh, one comprised of an array of sun-drenched men lounging in the surf.

"Well, I'm in good company," I thought to myself as I leafed through the magazine. "My interview is surrounded by naked men on the seashore." And then it struck me: *Greg would be proud.*

– 4 –

The Grounds on Which We Met:
Friendship and the Possible

Ed Madden

You are proof that it can happen and that it should.

Ralph Pomeroy
"A Tardy Epithalamium for E. and N."

I. Laguna Gloria Museum, Austin, Texas, October 1992

I first met Ed R. at his partner's memorial service on a bright autumn day in Austin, Texas. I remember holding my boyfriend's hand as a few people shared stories about Norbert. Norbert's sister started to read a memorial poem she'd written, but she broke down and someone else stepped in to finish it, while Ed held her hand and wept, and we all stood quiet in the sun and the fitful fall breeze, the museum grounds dappled with light. I didn't know anyone there except Brad, my first boyfriend. I had only recently come out, recently fallen into this, my first serious relationship with another man. And now I was meeting one of Brad's dearest friends at his partner's memorial. I felt strange—sidekick, interloper, the only one there who hadn't known Norbert. To Ed, however, there was nothing awkward about this. He hugged me, accepting me as part of his circle of friends.

Ed was my first gay friend.

By that I mean to say something more complicated than that statement might first suggest. I do not mean that he was my first friend who was gay. I had openly gay and lesbian friends and classmates at the University of Texas, where I was in grad school, but they had known me before I came out. There was something different about

On the Meaning of Friendship Between Gay Men

39

my meeting Ed, something different about the grounds on which we met. There was no *before* or *after* coming out in my relationship with Ed: I was simply the other Ed, Brad's boyfriend. My past might give me stories to tell, but that past self was not someone Ed had known. As a sexually active but deeply closeted gay man, I had also become acquainted with the sexual subcultures of the city, but the relationships forged in those spaces were often driven by secrecy and sex, even if they eventually became something other than that. Though a brief relationship or passion might develop, though a friendship of proximity and shared secrecy might offer itself, there was—at least for me—no sense of community in those networks of relation. It was a world fraught with silence and risk, not one of sociality and connection. While I might, with audacity, take a sexual partner to the fundamentalist church I attended and introduce him as "my friend," I employed the term as a euphemism.

So when I say Ed was my first gay friend, I emphasize the linkage of those two words, *gay* and *friend,* as well as the fact that for me Ed offered a welcome into a larger community. If Brad was my first "boyfriend" (I still remember the thrill I felt using that word to introduce him), then Ed was the first real friend I had in the gay community. Not only was there no *before* being out with him, as with my other friends, and not only did our friendship lack the context of secrecy and eroticism I associated with other gay acquaintances, there was also the sense that when Ed opened his arms and heart to me, he welcomed me into a new and quite different social world. There, on the grounds of Laguna Gloria Museum, gay friends, workplace colleagues, health care workers, and family members mingled, Ed and the absent Norbert, the center around which the moment turned.

Ed represented for me things I had never before imagined for myself: a community could exist in which I could be out—calmly, freely, without anxieties about who and when and how to tell—a community that could include all of my life. Norbert's memorial was proof. Within the next three years, a close friend from church would seek to have me excommunicated, other friends would drift away, my parents would reject me with letters more hurtful than I could have ever imagined, and my brother would ask me to lie to my grave. But, there with Ed, I could imagine something different. Ed was proof of what was possible: that a sexual (and sero-discordant) relationship could become a partnership, that sex could become love, that this could happen *and that it should.*

Ed also introduced me to what most gay men quickly discover: the chosen family of friends that replaces and sometimes exists in opposition to the traditional relationships of blood and marriage, kinship and obligation. Whenever I returned home for the holidays over the next three years, I felt more and more anxious and alienated, unable to be honest with my family. At the same time, I found greater and greater freedom and intimacy among my gay and lesbian friends. I remember a very queer Passover celebration, a mostly gay and mostly non-Jewish group of friends, drinking glass after glass of sweet kosher wines; I remember a wonderful Thanksgiving potluck, where a Whitman poem served as the requisite prayer; and I remember with great pleasure dinner at Ed's, his friends sitting around a television as we watched *All About Eve* (or was it *The Women?*)—a movie I was seeing for the first time while the men all laughed with recognition and familiarity, occasionally mimicking the lines.

A stereotype of gay culture? Perhaps. Outdated? Maybe. All I know is that I loved those evenings and loved those men. There was an intimacy and authenticity and openness that I have only found among other gay men. More important, it was part of my cultural education. Ed told me I couldn't be a "card-carrying fag" unless I'd seen certain movies—*Mommie Dearest, Whatever Happened to Baby Jane*—and he took it upon himself to show me at least a few of those films. It was Ed who took me to my first AIDS Walk through downtown Austin; it was Ed who went with me and Brad to New York City to see *Angels in America*; it was Ed who gave me my first (and only) tab of ecstasy—a New Year's Eve in 1995 that I will never forget.

Before I met Ed in 1992, before I came out, I was living in two worlds. There was my public self, the seminarian and graduate student from rural Arkansas who had recently broken up with a long-term girlfriend. And there was a private self, reading gay fiction (and throwing it all away before his parents or brother came to visit), meeting men for occasional brief and guilt-ridden sex. I spent time with male friends from church, one a grad student in business, the other a young minister. The MBA and I met on Friday afternoons for pizza and beer. My last Christmas card to him—a few years ago, long after we both graduated and he married—was returned with no forwarding address. The minister and I had more in common, including a genuine interest in intellectual sparring and theological issues, but I could not be fully myself with him either, and what intimacy I found with him would not allow for both my public and private selves. I craved the kind of understanding I would later find among gay friends.

Andrew Sullivan, discussing friendship in his 1998 book, *Love Undetectable,* says that a gay adolescent "doesn't really have a friend in the true sense of the term until he has a friend who knows and accepts the fact that he is gay" (p. 231). This friend is usually gay himself, says Sullivan, and this friendship has a deeper significance than other friendships, since it is only with that true and validating friend that we fully exist. Caught between two worlds, I couldn't find such a friend. Nor could I find a nonsexual intimacy that allowed me to be fully myself. On the one hand, I could meet a man at a sex party and develop an ongoing relationship with him, but be unable—when I introduced him as "my friend" at church—to explain how we met or what we had in common. On the other hand, I could hold hands and pray with a church friend, but never pray about the real anxieties driving my spiritual life. Sullivan says that sports provide an important chaperone for straight male friendships. As I discovered, beer and the Bible make great chaperones as well. More difficult for me was the way that eroticism and friendship might intersect. When I saw the minister playing shirts-and-skins basketball with the college boys from church, I carefully avoided looking at his sweaty, hairy chest, fearful of what my gaze might say about a friendship I truly valued. The erotic was a threat to this friendship, not simply in the way desire may threaten any friendship, but more because I knew that the fuller version of myself the erotic represented could never be acceptable in that friendship. It wasn't until I met Ed that I began to sense something of the many relational possibilities among gay men. And only then would I find the openness and intimacy I'd long craved.

II. Slick Rock Mountain, Near Brevard, North Carolina, October 2005

The leaves on the mountain hadn't turned yet, the summer too dry. Only the sumac and sassafras were gold and red, and there was a shiny bruise of purpled dogwood at the cabin's front door. Fast-forward thirteen years after Norbert's funeral: Brad and I broke up when I found a job in South Carolina, where I met Bert, my partner of over a decade. That fall, an older gay couple, Rod and Ed M. (yes, another Ed) invited Bert and me to their cabin in the mountains for the weekend. Just across the border of South Carolina, outside Brevard, we turned onto See Off Mountain Road, then up Slick Rock Drive. And there it was, their cabin, perched on the ridge of the mountain, the slopes falling sharply away on either side. They'd had it for years. They told us stories of storms, lightning, rattlesnakes, a (real) bear, a forest fire only yards away one summer, and a coastal hurricane sweeping in and ripping off the screen porch. They told us about the eerie quiet and isolation that envelopes the place when the valleys around it fill with clouds. When we sat quietly on that restored porch late one evening, there was a kind of openness among us—four men talking quietly beneath the moon—a quietness and an intimacy that had nothing to do with the vodka tonics or the moon, but just the way men could be, *should be,* together.

We met Rod and Ed at a dinner party where we were the youngest men present. Our friendship with them developed slowly—a Christmas party, a dinner out, a gift of flowers, cookies on the back step—almost as if we were all wooing each other. Both men are old enough to be our fathers or our uncles, but I hesitate to make those comparisons, mostly because my relationship with my own family has been one of loss, not support. I think such intergenerational friendships are critical to our understanding of ourselves—not just to our histories. Stuck in the bifurcated present moment of *Will and Grace* on television and marriage amendments on the ballot, we have limited possibilities for understanding our relationships and limited horizons for their realization. As Bert and I enter middle age and our thirteenth year together, we are still trying to figure out the nature of our relationship and fully realize its extravagant possibilities. It is not the same as a marriage, though I understand the importance of the current struggle for rights and security symbolized by marriage. We are learning from the men around us, our networks of friends.

Ed R. was my first gay friend. As someone struggling with difficulty to come to terms with my identity, facing the rejection of family and learning the risks and rewards of being out, I needed a friend like him. He taught me the languages and rituals of a new community. He was a model of what was possible, a mentor, a teacher of sorts ("But you are, Blanche, you are!"), a man who opened himself up to me, no questions asked. Just as I value the friendship of Ed in Austin for the way he introduced me to the community and culture of gay men, I also value my friendship with Rod and Ed in South Carolina, mentors and models in a different way, each of them offering an image of what was and still is possible. Rod and Ed's tenderness toward one another, their stories (both sordid and celebratory), as well as the many older men they introduce to us, some of them still deeply in the closet despite thirty or forty years of living with another man, help us to better understand and become ourselves. They offer a window into another way of becoming gay, as well as a continued lesson in the value of gay male friendships—the networks of intimacy, affection, and support that resist and exceed the prescribed relationships of family and obligation.

Bert and I spent one afternoon walking the mountain around the cabin, the rutted roads lined with sumac and aster, and the shadows filled with Galax. There was a joe-pye weed towering over the cabin's drive, and we imagined what the banks of rhododendron must look like in the spring. On one roadside bank, we found a small lilac and white striped flower, a strange bloom with its petals closed and attached at the tips. I looked it up in the guidebook in the cabin: a closed gentian, a blossom that won't open. Bees have to force their way into the blooms. The guidebook said they are rare, but there they were on the roads around the cabin.

When Rod tells us stories about the huge parties they used to throw, I feel I missed something, a moment when those parties and extended networks for friends were a crucial support system in a hostile culture. People came over a hundred miles to be there, from Charleston and Savannah and Charlotte. Maybe there's less of a need for those private parties and those closed networks of introduction and initiation now, as it is perhaps easier to be out. Rod and Ed, like so many other couples with their networks of friends, made a place for themselves and, in many ways, for us. Later that weekend, they took us to see the famous waterfalls of the area. Ed stopped on the trail, unable to make the long walk so soon after a recent illness, and Rod, still recuperating from feet broken in a fall from a ladder, went back when we reached the first falls. But Bert and I followed the trail, and when we stood in the spray of those last falls, we were so very grateful.

REFERENCES

Pomeroy, R. (1988). A tardy epithalamium for E. and N. In C. Morse and J. Larkin (Eds.), *Gay and Lesbian Poetry in Our Time: An Anthology* (pp. 315-316). New York: St. Martin's Press.
Sullivan, A. (1998). *Love undetectable: Notes on friendship, sex, and survival.* New York: Alfred A. Knopf.

– 5 –

Larry, Me, and "The Family"

Neil Kaminsky

It was last call.

The men scurried around the circular bar like hungry dogs: eyes darting, heads turning, sweat pouring. I stood there, Budweiser in hand. Distant. I was a veteran of the scene, but now retired. In a ten-year relationship, my agreement was to have sex with no one but my lover. So I didn't. Honest and trusting, I looked, I fantasized, but I went home alone.

The frenzy accelerated as the moments raced toward closing time. The sexual heat was palpable, thick and alive in the dark, smoky air. Desperate guys at a desperate moment. None of them wanted to be left standing when the music stopped.

And just then, it stopped for me. His eyes locked onto mine. I had never seen him before, yet he looked like I had always known him.

"Hi, my name is Larry," he smiled.

"I'm Neil," I answered, "and I just want you to know that I'm here to make friends but not have sex with anyone." I actually said that. It didn't displease him. Quite the contrary, it was like a breath of fresh

On the Meaning of Friendship Between Gay Men

47

air to him; the truth, direct, in your face honesty that he sorely missed in his new city of San Francisco. It was my new home also, and we were both refugees from the center of the universe: New York. We had both come to make life changes.

This was in the late fall of 1987, less than a year before my world crashed. August of 1988 was the darkest time of my life. I would discover that my lover had been living a clandestine life. I would learn that he had been with numerous guys throughout our "monogamous" relationship. I would acquire the abhorrent news that he was HIV positive. I would find out that he had had another boyfriend. He would leave me and move in with his new boyfriend—*into our apartment!*

Being unceremoniously heaved out of a fog of deceit after a decade is not good for the spirit or the mind. I stopped sleeping. I lost ten pounds. I moved robotically and whispered. I didn't understand English. I didn't know where I was though I knew where I needed to be—in an asylum. The psychiatrist at San Francisco General thought differently after my second emergency room visit: "You don't need a hospital, you need a new apartment."

She was right. Either move out or kill both of them. I chose to avoid San Quentin. Larry told me that there was an apartment available in his building on Grattan Street. I would be close to him. I moved.

It wasn't easy to let go of ten years. I loved Jack despite the scumbag I now knew him to be. Life had been lived in terms of *us.* Suddenly it was just me. Abruptly my past seemed fake and my future empty. Inconceivably, the man of my dreams had become the monster of my nightmares. And he had HIV. This man whom I loved (and hated) was going to die. In 1988, that was pretty much a given. I cried often and easily. Although Larry was a new friend, he was there when I needed him.

"You'll see, they'll find a cure," he told me one evening as I sobbed. "Jack will go the hospital, get a shot, and be fine." It sounded nice, but I knew better. Six years later I would give the eulogy at Jack's funeral.

After my first rendezvous with the psychiatric emergency room, I went into therapy. I saw a psychologist whose lover was dying of AIDS in the next room. (His office was in his house.) Probably not the best situation for me! Even worse, he didn't like me. I am sure of that to this day. My pining for Jack seemed to annoy him. Perhaps he didn't have it in him to empathize because of his own situation. Fragile and terrified, I kept seeing him. Talking did little, however, to close the ever-expanding abyss I was descending into. He referred me to a psychiatrist for medication.

Dr. Lepelto had an office on Van Ness Avenue near Fisherman's Wharf. The building looked early twentieth century: long, marble hallways, translucent glass doors, and a cold, dark sense about it. Not once did I see another human being in that building apart from Dr. Lepelto. I often wondered if it had been hit by a neutron bomb.

His private office felt just as strange. The waiting room was cemetery quiet, and the door to his inner office was always locked. I would speculate on whether he was seeing another patient, whether he was there at all, or even dead. But at the precise moment of our appointment, he would swing open the bolted door and usher me in.

Dr. Lepelto was strange looking, stranger sounding, and possessed the sensitivity of Mussolini—on a good day. But he was knowledgeable about psychopharmacology. He prescribed the antidepressant Elavil, which enabled me to sleep again. That was a blessing, and the beginning of my comeback. Slowly, my mind returned. I remembered what day it was. I could smile again.

I dated a bunch of guys. Crazy guys, of course, but I couldn't expect my defective ability to choose men to improve overnight. At least I wasn't living with them. Sex came back. Hot, yelling, sweaty, my next-door neighbor could hear us, sex. And whatever went on, I talked it over with Larry. Especially when my crazy boyfriends drove *me* crazy. Larry had endless patience, and I always felt better after speaking with him. His support was not of the Suzy Creamcheese variety. It was honest and deeply comforting. He understood the wisdom of feeling good, and saw the good in me. He bristled at unnecessary pain: "We are not here to suffer. And you don't deserve to suffer. You are a good person and you should be treated well." For a guy with tattered self-esteem, that was deliverance.

There were many frantic times yet to come, but Larry would be there to put me back together. Like the time one of my boyfriends ended our relationship on Market Street. I ran to Larry's house devastated. "It's all over," I exclaimed. "Not quite," he assured me. "Your relationship with that horrible man, who looks like my Aunt Mary, is over. Only that." Or the time I had an anxiety attack on the Muni subway. Out of nowhere I began to feel like I was losing it. My heart raced as my sight grew dim. I felt weak and clammy and thought I was about to die. Larry talked me down. Through the noise and throngs of people packed next to us in that tin can they call modern transportation, I could see Larry's kind face and hear his soothing voice. "You're okay. I'm with you. Nothing bad is going to happen. We're almost home."

Since we were so close, you may wonder if we ever had sex. We didn't. I can't say I was never attracted to him, however. I noticed his good looks the night we met. A month afterward we took a late night walk in Buena Vista Park. I knew I would do nothing. I was with Jack. But I wanted to fantasize. So I thought of us fooling around in that dark, isolated place as we walked together. That fantasy didn't last long. Tough, New York City Larry told me he was scared of the dark, and wanted to get out of the park immediately. We raced out, my lascivious thoughts disappearing under the bright illumination on Haight Street.

While I was still recovering from my depression, Ronnie, a friend of Larry's, moved to San Francisco from Chicago and in with Larry. Ronnie was a solidly nice guy, and I liked him immediately. Not very long after that, Craig, Ronnie's ex, moved here from St Louis. The three of them moved into a larger apartment in our building. Larry knew both of these guys from New York. Craig was shockingly hand-some, and the first time I saw him I was pleasantly overwhelmed. He was a sweet, funny guy who was easy to like—and easy on the eye.

I got the chance to relive an aspect of my childhood with these folks. When I was ten years old, my mother and I would visit Lizzy and Sophie in our six-story Brighton Beach apartment building. We'd drink tea and talk about everyone in the neighborhood. I was a young, budding *yenta.*

With these guys, weekend morning coffee paralleled teatime with Sophie and Lizzy. The topic of conversation was different, however. It was *men:* hot men, big-dicked men, fuck-him-but-then-run-from-him men, tricks gone wrong, fist fucking, and my latest dysfunctional boyfriend. We also derided, without mercy, some of the characters we saw in the bars. We, well, mostly me, christened them Crab Nose, Blow Job Mary, Mr. Death, The Drunken Psychologist, The Gray Eagle, Plaid Man, and Blond Monsters 1, 2, 3, and 4. Those were divine moments.

In the months that followed, friends grew on trees. There was a whole mess of ex–New Yorkers gravitating west and finding a home in our ever-expanding circle of happy refugees. We seemed to smell each other out, and if one of us met someone, he was introduced to the rest of us. Sometimes two friends moved out together. Danny appeared from New York with his roommate Felix. Some of Larry's other friends showed up: Angel, Gilbert, and Richard. It was wonderful how much we were all in sync, and how effortlessly friendships developed. We called ourselves "The Family."

Although no one forced any of us to move to California, we loved to complain about San Francisco and the airhead boys. Perhaps this helped solidify our group. Of course we socialized with others, but there was something more comfortable and familiar when relating to a fellow New Yorker. You knew where you stood with him. California boys had to be translated. Larry and I both had bizarre experiences with them. They seemed to speak another language and have a value system we couldn't understand. We were particularly dismayed about their incredible ability to flake out and not have a clue that they had done anything wrong. It drove Larry and me crazy.

Larry came to dislike San Francisco. I liked it, despite the flakes. I was also thrilled by its beauty: the hills, the pastel colors, and the fog. I felt calmer in San Francisco. I appreciated the Castro and felt privileged to be part of that community.

I especially loved these friendships in my "small gay town." It was difficult to walk through the Castro without running into someone I knew. On Friday nights, we'd congregate at Badlands bar, and by 11 p.m. there was a crowd of us. When I traveled, I couldn't wait to get back. I even sent cards, "gushy" cards, as Larry called them. I basked in the knowledge that San Francisco and my friends were waiting for me. Holidays were difficult after Jack. But with Larry and the other guys around, the pain was mitigated. I never remember being alone during those times.

There were many social gatherings. Eddie and Lee, who were a couple, hosted dinner parties in their gorgeous home in the Oakland hills. The views were fantastic, the food wonderful, and the company divine. Danny and Felix lived in a small apartment near Noe and Market. Their parties were on a much less grand scale, but no less fun.

A party I'll never forget was Larry's thirty-second birthday. I decided it would be a surprise. It took place in my home. My studio apartment was tiny but it had a closet the size of a small city. It covered the length of the room with two doors, one on each side. When my friend Gordon came to live with me from New York, he literally slept in it for a month. I arranged for the other Family members to hide there while Ronnie and Craig brought poor, unsuspecting Larry to my house. I told him that only the four of us were going to go out for dinner to celebrate.

Picture this: A small studio apartment with ten grown men hiding in a closet. Not a sound coming from it. There sits Larry on my couch thinking he's with only the three of us. At a prearranged signal, when I said, "This is a nice night," out came ten laughing, screaming queens. It reminded me of the circus. Larry jumped up in shock. He got into a combat stance. For a microsecond his brain couldn't comprehend what was happening. He looked ridiculous and we all laughed. He was a good sport, and also found it funny once he realized that he wasn't about to be clobbered.

Larry, Ronnie, and Craig eventually moved to a three-bedroom apartment on States Street, very close to the Castro. I remained on Grattan Street.

When the Loma Preita earthquake hit on October 17, 1989, I retreated to their house. I had been home at the time. I arrived early that day from work and was inspired to do my laundry. That feeling comes infrequently, so I was hastening, fearful it would dissipate. My laundry never got done—that evening anyway.

It was about 5 p.m. For the first second I wasn't sure what was going on. I felt a little jerk under my feet. I questioned out loud, "What the hell is this?" But before I could answer, I realized exactly what it was. The slight movement transformed into a violent, rapid shaking. It was so fierce that my apartment looked blurry. Glasses smashed onto the floor, books went flying, shelves collapsed, and my windows rattled angrily.

As my apartment was coming down on me, I did exactly what I was told *never* to do: run my ass down three fights of steps and out onto the street. To hell with getting under a doorway arch, I thought. I saw the words "buried alive" in my mind's eye, and I was gone. Dashing down three flights of moving stairs is terrifying, as is passing a collapsing wall. But I made it out unscathed, then ran directly to Larry's.

Larry and Craig were home. Soon Ronnie arrived, having walked from downtown. Others came over. I went from feeling alarmed to feeling safe. How could anything bad happen now? I also have to admit that I was having a little fun. I was with my buddies, living through a major event. How much more exciting than doing my laundry!

Larry's phone was working, so I called my mother. She was living in Florida. She and my aunt Tillie were freaking out, having seen the whole mess on TV. It looked like Dresden. I assured her that I wasn't hurt.

Loma Preita was only one of many memorable events. The Family took trips to the Napa Valley. I hiked with Ronnie and Larry and Craig through the gorgeous countryside of the East Bay. I went with Gordon to Virginia City in Nevada, and loved the feeling of pretending I was in the Old West.

We also spent lots of time in the bars. Those were glorious nights of boys, beer, and bawdiness. We went home with crazy tricks and somehow survived to tell the stories. Frequently we had 3 a.m. breakfasts at Orphan Andy's or at Sparky's on Church Street. There were also sex club escapades. A group of us once visited a house of debauchery paradoxically named The Church. Larry didn't take his pants off in public so he waited downstairs. But he wasn't alone for long. A very large young man found him and gave him a bear hug that almost killed him. He named the guy "Papushka." I don't know how to describe this guy other than to say he was definitely a "Papushka."

There's no forever. Passing is the nature of living. But ours arrived unjustly too soon, and with obscene cruelty. Death first revealed itself in the outer corners of my world. It started with strangers, men I simply recognized as familiar faces in the Castro. I saw changes that made me gasp. A hunk one day; a disabled, gaunt apparition the next. Then I'd see the man's face, restored to its original, on the obituary page in the *Bay Area Reporter.*

When Larry told me that Craig had lung cancer, I knew he was going to die. The picture of that moment is still painfully clear. Craig had been sounding hoarse for weeks. I came into their house and Larry ushered me into his bedroom. "He has lung cancer," he said with a half-pained smile. My mother had that same smile whenever she had horrible news. It wasn't many weeks later when I received the phone call. "Neil," Larry's voice was clear and serious, "Craig has passed." "Passed?" I questioned myself stupidly. As in passed away, as in dead at the age of thirty, as in I would never see him again? Craig had HIV. That I already knew. It had been a shock when I first found out. But I thought, or rather wanted to believe, that somehow he'd be okay.

It was in the Pendulum bar that Eddie disclosed to me that he had HIV. He was heavyset, full of energy, how could he have HIV, I wondered? But he did, and he also would change. I would see him and Lee in the Castro. But now Eddie remained in the car while Lee went shopping. He didn't get out because he no longer had the energy to stand.

At the last get-together at his home in the Oakland hills, he was too weak to even sit up. He lay on a makeshift bed on a couch. It was in the living room so he could be with us. He had a bottle next to him that he used to urinate in. Spiritually, he was the same man, full of kindness and love and not one iota of self-pity. He stayed with us through the conversation as best he could. He talked, he even laughed, but he didn't have much strength or endurance. I watched him closely. When it was time to leave, I hugged him. I felt only bones, and it made me sad and sick to my stomach.

A week later Eddie had a stroke and was hospitalized. Larry and I visited him. His mother was also there. We all talked in the most normal of ways. We tried to include Eddie as he squirmed around, his vacant eyes migrating up into his head. But he wasn't with us any longer. I felt cold and dead as I bore witness to this unspeakable tragedy. Looking at Eddie's mother, the pain was unbearable. At one point Larry and I left the room to get water. As Larry leaned down to the water fountain, he burst into tears. I touched his back, trying to console him, but I was a zombie.

A week later Eddie was dead. I attended the memorial in his home. It was held in that beautiful living room in the Oakland hills, the same room where we had the parties, the same place I had visited him as he lay on that makeshift bed. All of The Family was there. His ashes were in an urn. Angel, always mischievous, was no different even then. He beckoned me with a naughty twinkle as he opened the urn. I told him not to do it as I looked in at Eddie's ashes.

"I was the love of his life," Angel would proclaim to me at Badlands. "Come, let's go away, just the two of us, Nelson," as he liked to call me. It was always in jest. But there was a subtext to this. Angel knew Larry long before I did, and Larry's friendship with me bothered him. It manifested in this behavior when he called me Nelson, or when he made disparaging remarks about Larry when he wasn't there. I didn't like that, and so I had difficulty liking Angel. It never bothered Larry, however. "That was Angel," he told me.

Larry stood by Angel *like* an angel when he was dying. It started with a pain in his rib that was, in fact, cancer. He was also HIV positive. Larry was living with him at the time. Angel's mother moved in and they both took care of him together. I remember seeing Angel right before he passed. The light in his soul was gone. I saw a somber Angel I had never met.

Not long after that, Lee would die, then Hector, then Felix, then Richard. It wouldn't stop. The bodies piled up. Memorials became routine. Phone calls, announcing the latest passing, were common. Death infiltrated every crevice of my existence. I grew weary, sad, lost.

The Family disappeared.

After Angel's death, Larry was clinically depressed. He couldn't eat or shit and lost a great deal of weight. Soon he would tell his crazy boss to go to hell, begin Zoloft, and move as far as he could from San Francisco: Washington, DC.

I put on a good face for this. I tried to convince myself that it was only a matter of time before I'd join him in Washington. But Larry's leaving was a watershed moment in my life. My best friend would now be on the opposite coast.

The rest of the living joined a large exodus: Ronnie escaped to Denver, Danny also moved to Washington DC, Gordon got a job offer in New York and took it, and Gilbert moved to Washington, then to New York. I remained behind, left on a sinking ship. I just couldn't get myself to bale.

Larry said to me a few days ago that he wants his life back.

I want something back also.

We have been apart for over a decade and haven't missed a beat. We talk all the time and are as close as ever, although I miss his physical presence terribly.

Larry was with his lover for seven years, a man he met in Washington but with whom he had been exceedingly unhappy for most of that time.

It bothered me that he wasn't happy. The paradox didn't escape me either: how could a man who told *me* that we are not here to suffer remain in a relationship that makes *him* miserable? I guess love, or the illusion thereof, can do strange things to the best of us. But all of this came to a crashing halt two weeks ago. I was having my usual weekend conversation with Larry when he told me that they had broken up.

"It's over Neil. I'm moving. I have a new place."

My first impulse was to soothe him. No one spends seven years with a person and leaves without some sadness. So I tried to comfort him. But there was something in his voice that told me he didn't need comforting. It was the sound of hope. It made me joyous.

Since that conversation, his spirits have further brightened. During our last talk he even joked that his gray hair is turning black again. And that's when he told me that he wants his life back. I have no doubt he's going to get it. And me?

I fell in love in San Francisco. Virgilio and I are going on six years. We now live in LA. We have good jobs. We're healthy. We love one another. But something is missing, unsettled, deeply unsettled, and eats away at my soul every day of my life.

I want what no longer is.

I don't suppose I'll be getting that back.

Circuitries of Friendship: Camaraderie and Collectivity on the Gay Dance Floor

Vincent A. Lankewish

For my friends on the dance floor—past, present, and yet to come.

Circuit, n., **1. a.** The line, real or imaginary, described in going round any area; the distance round; the compass, circumference, containing lines or limits. **2. b.** *fig.* Sphere of action, etc. **3. a.** The action of going or moving around or about; a circular journey, a round.

The Oxford English Dictionary

i. Sparklers in the Darkness

[L]ike sparks in the darkness, . . .
burning down forever and forever.

James Taylor
"There We Are" (1977)

It is June 1999, and I am with my friends on the dance floor of Club Octagon in Manhattan for "Climax," an annual New York Pride weekend event at which lesbian disc jockey Susan Morabito spins for

On the Meaning of Friendship Between Gay Men

a crowd of about 1,000 gay men. My buddy Brian from New Orleans worked hard to get us tickets to this sold-out evening. Disco diva Donna Summer's club hit "Con Te Partiro" ("I Will Go With You")— a remix of opera singer Andrea Bocelli's blockbuster—is reverberating throughout the club, when a group of men begin to light sparklers, one after the other, until soon the entire octagonal room is illuminated with these wands of flickering fire. For just a few minutes, everyone is mesmerized, if not transfigured, as they behold this scene of beauty. I quickly find my friend Rick and exclaim, "Wouldn't Carolyn love this? A truly 'Paterian' moment!" Rick concurs that our mutual friend Carolyn, the author of a ground-breaking book about the Victorian aesthete Walter Pater, would be ecstatic if she had witnessed these sparks in the darkness. Then, one by one, the sparklers begin to fade, leaving only remembered traces of their presence. I wistfully recall Pater's famous words in the "Conclusion" of *The Renaissance*: "To burn always with this hard, gem-like flame, to maintain this ecstasy is success in life" (1873, p. 219).

Out on the dance floor in a group huddle with cherished pals, I pause for a few moments and wonder: What would Pater, a writer whose work has figured prominently in my own scholarship, have to say about this explosion of sensory and artistic pleasure? Has he miraculously been resurrected to preside over this evening's revelries? It is as if he is here with me, taking delight in the spectacle of lights, colors, sounds, movement, bodies, or the faces of one's friends. I can't help thinking that Pater is reaching across time and space with his queer hand and touching me, my companions, and all of the other gay men in my midst.

Without discounting the hierarchies—gender, racial, ethnic, and economic—and the "body fascism" that, as Michelangelo Signorile sees it, govern gay culture in general and, more specifically "the circuit," as the national and international network of gay dance parties has come to be known, I meditate for a few moments more as I survey the dance floor. The club is packed with men and a small, but visible, number of women, all of whom, at least for these few minutes, seem to have found that "happy spot," the discovery of which Pater sees as so crucial to permitting people to "burst into life." I think about the vital, life-affirming, sex-positive messages promoted by gay dance club culture, especially within the context of HIV and AIDS. I see many couples dancing together, but the multiple groupings I observe suggest that for many of those in attendance, the circuit is not just about coupling, monogamy, "marriage," nor even necessarily sexuality—although that, of course, significantly figures in the scene—but also very much about friendship, camaraderie, and collectivity.

In brief, "Climax" 1999 helps bring back to mind something that I—as a gay man who came out in 1980 and, thus, briefly knew a time before AIDS—seem to forget too easily: not simply the thrill of tricking, anonymous sex, and the unexpected intimacies that these encounters could yield, but, rather, the ties that have bound my friends and me across the past two decades; the circuitous routes that have brought us into one another's lives; the circles that we have traveled over time to arrive here tonight; the crisscrossings, hellos and goodbyes, points of departure, and points of return that have served as the hardwiring of this network. I remember those bonds, those journeys, those orbits, those intersections, and even those paths that have never converged as I observe the world of friendships being endlessly created and re-created around me.

ii. Entering the Dance Competition

> I'm coming out of hiding.
> I'm coming out of hiding.
>
> James Lee Stanley and James Melamed
> "Coming Out of Hiding" (1984)

My tendency toward the cerebral, rather than the affective, has always been a bit of a curse when trying to move to the music and blur the distinction, as W.B. Yeats would have it, between dancer and the dance. My friend Wayne affectionately mocks me whenever I begin to deconstruct what I would call "the text" of the evening. "Friends," he has so often remarked, "don't let friends use polysyllabic words on the dance floor!" Translation: Shut up and dance! That said, a certain degree of history and self-reflection is necessary for me to explicate the shifts in my relationship to the dance floor over the past twenty-five years.

My story begins in the early 1980s. As an undergraduate at NYU, I came out within a few months of moving into the Brittany Residence Hall in Greenwich Village. My roommates Martin, John, and Jary opened the door to worlds—intellectual, cultural, and social—that heretofore had existed only in my imagination: Three Lives Bookstore, Fran Leibowitz and other lesbian and gay writers, *The New York Native,* camp classics, *Evita, Dreamgirls,* Marie's Crisis, fag hags, Uncle Charlie's, Julius, Cahoots, The Works, gay dances at Columbia University, and, of course, the clubs. Crisco Disco, The Underground, Limelight, The River Club, Studio 54 in its decline, The Saint in its ascent—these were some of the popular venues for dancing at the time. But while literature, film, musical theatre, piano bars, and cruising were aspects of gay culture that I learned to navigate over time, the dance floor remained an enigmatic and uncomfortable space for someone who suffered from a morbid self-consciousness and was ill at ease in his body—someone, that is, like me.

The initial promotional ad for the opening of The Saint in 1980 asserted, "Since the beginning of recorded history, the male members of the species have joined together in ritual dance. Adorned, semi-naked with rhythm instruments, they used this tribal rite to celebrate their gods and themselves. The Saint has been created to perform the mystery—to continue the rite." Nonetheless, both the mission of this club—which I visited once while at NYU—and the release that my friends enjoyed while engaging in ritual dance painfully eluded me. Only many years later did I learn that the awkwardness of my movement—or lack thereof—became the object of parody. One member of our circle, I was informed, inaugurated the "Vinny Dance Contest" behind my back. I still wince at the thought of this cruelty, but when I picture myself then and now, I, too, have to acknowledge the comical figure that I must have cut in the disco years. Although I had come out, I nonetheless remained hidden on the dance floor, to myself and to those around me. It would take well over a decade for me to burst into life and, in turn, to realize that I could sparkle in the dark. In the interim, however, I struggled to discover an authentic self and thereby escape the daily fabrication and performance of identity that had served as my survival mechanism since my adolescence.

My initial attempt to return to the dance floor at the June 1997 "Climax" event was disastrous, at best. Although I had completed my doctorate just a few months before and thought myself in exceptionally good spirits, I was in no way prepared for what felt like an all-out assault on my senses and, more importantly, my ego. I met up early in the evening with my friends Martin and John, whom I had known for nearly twenty years, and several of their friends. I had a beer and danced for a while with this group, which did its best to make me feel welcome, but I simply could not shake off the dis-ease that undermined my greatest efforts to get into some kind of groove. Moreover, I felt woefully inadequate when I surveyed all of the handsome faces and well-muscled bodies around me. I soon absented myself from the dance floor and climbed the stairs to the club's second story, which allowed me to observe the crowd from above.

That evening represented not only my first real venture back into a club, but also my first experiment with ecstasy. When it began to kick in, I backed myself against a wall to keep from falling over. The first ten minutes seemed like an eternity, as wave after crashing wave of MDMA hit me. Then, suddenly, I felt as if I'd been lifted onto a cloud. I wanted to let go and enjoy this new sensation, but my obsessive need to be in control at all times kept me from fully submitting to the experience. Instead, I stood at the railing overlooking the dance floor and simply watched in amazement the sea of shirtless men below enjoying themselves without inhibition. About midway through the night, Susan Morabito played a club remix of Jon Secada's "Too Late, Too Soon." When the song's refrain started, everyone sang along with joy and exuberance. No matter that the song is about a man who discovers his girlfriend in bed with another man: the crowd had taken up "Too Late, Too Soon" and transformed it into an anthem that connected everyone—friends, lovers, and strangers—for that moment. Standing on the sidelines, I remained thoroughly disconnected from all that I beheld—an observer, rather than a participant. As morning approached, I left the club, certain that this would be my first and last experience of "the circuit" about which I'd heard so much. I didn't even try to find my friends to say goodbye.

iii. Remembering My Thousand Knights

> It's time we told each other stories (stories)
> Of our thousand nights.

Glenn Schellenberg and John Greyson
"Scheherazade (Tell a Story)"
Zero Patience (1993)

In his essay "The School of Giorgione," Pater (1873) offers a compelling and moving description of the life-giving forces of "play." He remarks with respect to leisure time that

> [o]ften such moments are really our moments of play, and we are surprised at the unexpected blessedness of what may seem our least important part of time; not merely because play is in many instances that to which people really apply their own best powers, but also because at such times, the stress of our servile, everyday attentiveness being relaxed, the happier powers in things without are permitted free passage, and have their way with us. (p. 166)

In February 1998, less than a year after "Climax," I finally began to enjoy my own moments of play and to allow "the happier powers in things without" to have their way with me. Over the next three years, I would cultivate an appreciation of the pleasures of the circuit scene and the gay dance floor in general and, as a result of the friendships nurtured over time at parties and clubs across the country, come to terms with the multiple—and, for me, richly significant—meanings of the word "circuit" itself. Having just accepted a position as an assistant professor of English at Penn State-University Park, I felt particularly self-confident at the time. That I had lost a significant amount of weight and had been working out regularly only heightened this feeling. Attending the White Party at Roseland in Manhattan and a follow-up event at Club Octagon the next evening—both with the same friends whom I'd joined for that catastrophic, anticlimactic "Climax"—dramatically altered my perspective of the circuit.

For me, its magnetism lay in three distinct, but often overlapping, phenomena: aesthetic experience, erotic connection, and companionship. The sensory stimuli of a party or a club—venue, theme, décor, music, performances, crowd, clothing, sartorial accoutrements, and costumes, along with the faces, flesh, and muscles of men of all ages, types, and sizes—shaped many of my marvelous nights and dawns. In my mind's eye, I can see myself making my way across the dance floor at Club Octagon for "Climax" 1998 wearing a silver boater hat that led me to my friend Drew, whom I credit and thank for exponentially multiplying the possibilities of loving friendship in my life. I see myself at the Pavilion in the Pines, looking up at the legendary chandelier while out with Marc and Alan and Keith and Al and

Adam, my housemates from 582 Fire Island Boulevard. And on the sand after the Y2K party in South Beach, watching the sun come up over the ocean with my buddies Rick and Chuck. Or at Black and Blue at the Olympic Stadium in Montreal, looking up at the dome and feeling as if I were traveling in a spooky spaceship with my gang to galaxies unknown. Or those other truly colorful events, like the Red Party 1999 in Columbus, Ohio, bumping and grinding on top of a box with a guy named Bill to Nancy Griffith's "Late Night Grand Hotel"; Blue Ball 2000 in Philadelphia, dancing with a muscle daddy; and Cherry 5 in Washington, DC, hooking up with a twink; and Halloween 2001 in NOLA, when I began to recognize the beginning of the end. Today, these moments and men seem like so many pages of ancient history, but their transience is counteracted by the longevity of the friendships forged over the three-year period from 1998 to 2001, which I regard as my circuit salad days.

Although the Red Party is generally considered the "first" circuit party, as it originated in the mid-1970s, the Gay Men's Health Crisis (GMHC) in New York sponsored the ironically named "Morning Party" on the beach of the Fire Island Pines each August from 1982 until 1998. I feel fortunate to have attended the last such party, and, thus, to have had a part, however small, in a history whose significance I did not know as an undergraduate, but that would resonate for me in the years to come. Three moments of friendship from that August afternoon on the beach remind me that I have gained something from learning to dance that will endure, that will be with me wherever I go: first, my friend John's insistence that when the disc jockey, Buck, played Lighthouse Family's "High," we all find one another and collectively immerse ourselves in the song's sentiments: "And at the end of the day, / . . . [W]e'll remember it was me and you;" second, dancing with my friend Martin to the party's penultimate song in which James Taylor urged us to "[s]hower the people you love with love, / Tell them the way that you feel." (I was just about to move to State College, Pennsylvania, and sobbed on his shoulder, as I suddenly appreciated the timelessness of our friendship.); and, third, the final song of the afternoon, "(I've Had) The Time of My Life," which spoke volumes about a day on the dance floor with my friends.

iv. Don't Leave Me This Way

I can't stay alive
Without your love.

Kenneth Gamble, Cary Gilbert, and Leon Huff,
"Don't Leave Me This Way" (1975)

Over the past five years, circuit queens have been lamenting the loss of the tribal, ecstatic connection between men whose recovery was The Saint's mission. In "Whatever Happened to the Circuit Party: Diary of an Aging Circuit Queen," Alan Brown (2000) nostalgically remarks: "Like Norma Desmond with seratonin depletion, I tend to overly-romanticize my early days on the party circuit." Brown attributes some of his grief to a generation gap. "Young gay men don't seem to derive much social utility from the idea of a party circuit," he comments. "One generation's lifestyle is anathema to the next generation. . . . The party circuit was an idealized social construct more than anything else, and perhaps it is also the case that the old vaporware has gone up in smoke, as it eventually must" (p. 66).

Brown is not alone in his belief that some, if not much, of the queer magic of the circuit scene seems to have vanished over the past few years. Cyber-gays who post to "Circuit Party Insanity," a LISTSERVE mailing list for circuit enthusiasts, for example, have themselves posed questions like, "Remember the time when the CIRCUIT was amazing?" or "Is the circuit too big now anyway?" His experience of loss notwithstanding, Brown (2000) retains his faith in the possibilities of regeneration that the circuit represents and has asserted that "[d]espite predictions to the contrary, the party scene is here to stay" (p. 69).

In assessing the powers of the circuit, Brown (2001) observes:

> One of my favorite things to do at a party is to climb up on a platform and look down over the party from above. From far enough away, the sea of bodies becomes a single mass of human protoplasm, like a living organism. What is your contribution to the party? A fabulous costume? Greeting a stranger? Massaging a friend's head and shoulders? Running for water? Outbound expressions of camaraderie are always welcome, but perhaps the biggest contribution you can make is to approach the experience

with a sense of adventure, self-awareness, openness to new people, new music, and new energy, and a commitment to the collective experience. (n.p.)

The advice that Brown offers seems—to me, at least—remarkably Paterian, urging new generations of gay men to make the most of every moment on the dance floor. I know that I can never relive the night when I saw those sparklers burn, nor any other such nights, for that matter. However, I can always recall the camaraderie and collectivity that my friends and I have shared and the ways that the pyrotechnics of the circuit turned the darkness of my dance floor days in college into a perpetually glowing flame.

REFERENCES

Brown, A. (2000). Whatever happened to the party circuit?: Diary of an aging circuit queen. *Circuit Noize, 26,* 66-69.
Brown, A. (2001). Partying for your life. *Black and blue festival program book.* Montreal, Quebec: BBCM Foundation.
Pater, W. (1873/1986). *Walter Pater: Three major texts (the renaissance, appreciations* and *imaginary portraits).* W. E. Buckler (Ed.). New York: New York University Press.

PART IV:
ON FRIENDSHIP AND SEXUALITY

– 7 –

A Towel and a TV

Michael E. Thomas II

During those last few minutes before I'm about to meet a romantic stranger for the first time, there's a foreboding dialogue that goes on in my head. One Saturday, I was thinking: "What am I doing and why am I doing it?"

What I was doing was meeting Alexander Ivanov, the twenty-four-year-old Bulgarian, who lived in Washington DC. From his photos, I expected us to have a casual, fun time during his weekend visit to NYC. For some reason, if plans go too smoothly, I get a little suspicious. Is it too good to be true?

My first contact with him sprang from a simple day of perusing a Web site called "Gaydar." The site makes it easy to hunt for sex, by location, all over the world. The New York City room is always full, packed with men of all sizes, shapes, and colors. Yet somehow, I felt a strange pull away from the NYC rooms, almost as if I knew that I'd find the right person somewhere else. I popped into the Washington DC room and found a photo of Alexander standing by a pool, wearing

On the Meaning of Friendship Between Gay Men

a dark Speedo, showing off a smooth, chiseled body. My heart leaped. I messaged him:

"Hot photos! Do you ever get to NYC? I'd love to play with you sometime."

His reply marked the first of a string of those "too good to be truisms:"

"You are hot, too! I'm coming to NYC next weekend."

How weird. What were the chances of him coming here in just a few days for a visit? We began sending messages back and forth. I offered to let him stay at our place. He thanked me and accepted the offer. My boyfriend Christian seemed agreeable, but I later decided against it. Even though Christian made it clear it was fine for him to come and that he liked his photos as well, I knew that I would want Alexander all to myself. Plan B was for me to put him up in a hotel room. Once I assured him that I really wanted to and that it would give us the privacy we needed, he agreed.

On Saturday, Alexander called me before leaving home. He was traveling by bus and expected to arrive around 5 p.m. near Madison Square Garden, where we planned to meet. I boarded the A train from uptown Manhattan in time to arrive at 34th Street. Having timed it almost exactly to the minute, I walked above ground to find two new voicemail messages on my cell phone. The first was from Alexander, telling me the bus had faced heavy traffic and that he'd be late. The second was from Malcolm, a young Australian guy whom I had recently met. He called to say that he had just finished watching a matinee performance of *The Boy from Oz* and that he loved it. After listening to the two messages, I called Alexander, during which time— shockingly—Malcolm happened to appear right in front of me. We hugged and marveled at the coincidence. When I told him I was waiting for a friend to arrive from DC, he suggested that, in the meantime, we go have coffee and catch up.

Meanwhile, Alexander and I kept checking in with each other, realizing what little progress he was making through the traffic. He said he thought he might be in New Jersey. I asked if he saw any part of the New York City skyline and he said no. I feared a long wait, but at least I knew he was on his way. When Malcolm and I parted, I looked for ways to entertain myself. This became its own adventure. I met a sixteen-year-old blond kid from California with his mother and helped them map out an evening of sightseeing. I took them on their first subway ride and loved the lad's fascination with it all. I walked about town looking at the enormous crowds of holiday tourists and typical NYC street weirdoes. The energy in the city was full and rich and my anticipation for meeting Alexander grew. I decided to wait at Penn Station, where I could sit on the floor and play Snake II on my cell phone.

It was around 7:00 p.m. when I noticed Alexander—tall, blond, and gorgeous—walking toward me, his eyes shifting rapidly from side to side, scanning to find the shaved head brown guy. When he saw me, I rapidly scanned his face to see if he was as pleased as I was. He seemed to be. We kissed. He then wished me a Merry Christmas as he gave me a handsomely wrapped gift. I would sniff the Aveda scented lotion and hand cream inside for weeks to come. I thanked him.

Since he was hungry, I took him to Rice and Beans in Hell's Kitchen. We clicked so naturally, both of us talking freely and with rapt attention. Just looking at him was sheer ecstasy. He was the perfect Eastern European man, gorgeous beyond words. His bone structure and facial features were sharp and fine; he had dark brown eyes, which contrasted with his pale skin; he was tall but moved with all the fluidity and energy of a young boy. During our meal, we made plans for later that evening. Our conversation revealed a few fun facts: I learned that he was born in Bulgaria on August 4th, the same day as my ex-boyfriend Billy, and that he had come out to his mother over the telephone. We shared stories of our family's misconceptions about being gay. Alexander seemed fascinated by my description of myself as sensitive, emotional, and intellectual. He said that he identified with those qualities.

Before we left the restaurant, we agreed to meet some of my other friends, including Malcolm, at a bar called Therapy. After dinner, Alexander and I took a cab up to our hotel, The West Side Inn, on 107th Street. During the ride, I enjoyed the delicate way in which he held my hands and snuggled a bit with me, displaying a tender and gentle soul.

Once at the hotel, after walking aimlessly back and forth between the tight, dark little hallways, we finally found our room. As we entered, my heart sank. It had one small, rickety bed, no cover, just a sheet and one folded down blanket. And there was nothing else, except a towel and a TV.

The entire building was old and the room was no bigger than a large closet with layers and layers of caked-on paint. There was one overhead light with a long dirty string attached. It shone so brightly with the most putrid florescent bulb that we could little tolerate its overbearing, greenish hue. The room was disgusting. But to think how such ugliness could transform into magnificent beauty by the sheer force of romantic perfection that was about to unfold little by little between us. Just beneath that ghastly light, we started to kiss passionately when Alexander interrupted with, "I've got an idea."

He turned the light off and opened the shade overlooking a view of the backside of some old Upper West Side apartments. The only redeeming quality from this angle was that the trickle of light would radiate off our naked bodies. After fastening the shades to open fully, we stripped each other and kissed. I hungered for his thin, pink, and shapely lips. I could taste the scent and flavor of his tongue, which lingered in my mind the entire weekend. His beauty overwhelmed me. Everything about him melded together in a poetic integration, making me dizzy. He became mine and I became his, and only his, during this magical day, a day in which fantasy became reality.

His name derived from one of my favorite heroes, Alexander the Great, who once conquered and ruled the same region where he was born. Standing before me, Alexander the Great was reincarnated. His mother broke a strict family tradition by giving him the name of one of history's greatest conquerors. Tonight he ruled still. He reminded me of those beautiful Eastern European boys I fantasized about. His voice, his accent, his eyes, his cheekbones, his lips, his wide hips, his well-proportioned, muscled body, his broad shoulders, and his beautiful, uncut penis awed me.

This first time together in the room, we had sex. The second, and third, and fourth times, we would be making love! But for now, we were off to the bar. During the cab ride, Alexander answered a phone call. As he spoke with his friend, he was describing some of his evening thus far, including the condition of his little hotel room. He said, "The only thing I have in that room is a towel and a TV!" The cabdriver could not resist reacting. He started to laugh and said, "Only in New York. A towel and a TV!"

While at Therapy, I met some of my friends—Kingsley, Brandon, Brad, and Malcolm. Some of Alexander's friends were there as well. I was glowing, side by side and arm in arm with the most beautiful guy there. It was fun to talk, laugh, and socialize with everyone, but the highlight of the evening was kissing and playing with Alexander. From there, we went to *the* gay dance club, Roxy. What a time! Alexander was so sweet. I thought it was considerate of him to keep checking in with me saying, "We can leave whenever you want. If you want to go, that's fine with me if you're tired." We left around 3:00 a.m.

Back at the room, it was like returning home together. Somehow its ugliness seemed cozy, even cute. Alexander spoke about how charming the building was as an artifact. It wasn't long before we again stripped each other and rolled all over the bed. We made love and it was good. We kissed and played with each other's bodies as if we owned each other. And indeed, we did, if only for this one day. I was all his and loved giving myself to him, and he was all mine, telling me that I was his. I took him again and again. Sleeping with him, lying in his arms all night, waking up, and making love with him again in the morning made an already perfect day together seem magical, even heavenly.

Before we parted that Sunday afternoon, I thought about our little hotel room. It seemed fine for it to have been so bare since, in contrast, it made Alexander's beauty all the more striking.

Now, it was time for me to head home to my boyfriend. I felt depressed and doubtful about our open relationship, so frequently boasted about to our friends; I felt a little empty and angst-ridden to be torn away from Alexander; I started to think about how sexual obsession and the compulsive behavior that follows, makes everything around it seem romantic, until the ritual ends that is, at which point everything is left bare and plain and impoverished; I felt like the towel and TV: folded, washed up, waiting until the next person could watch me and turn me on.

Eventually Alexander and I became friends, shaped by the more customary means of getting to know someone: we saw movies, met for brunch, took in people-watching on the Upper West Side, exchanged serious and platonic e-mail messages, and showed a glimpse here and there of emotional vulnerability. My heroic, conquering Alexander became human. He spoke with me about dead-end dates, new boyfriends, and his mixed emotions about his career in retail. I spoke with him about my unhappy life with my boyfriend and about my yearning to write, despite my fears. Across state lines, playful text messages amassed on our cell phones like shiny little secret gold coins, too precious to ever spend, as blessed in the outgoing box as much as in the incoming one:

"Just thinking about you."

"Hey, what are you doing?"

"Sending you the biggest kiss."

"I love you."

"I love you, too."

"Hey, thanks for your really great advice last night."

 "That's what friends are for. You do the same for me."

"I'm sorry, Madonna is still fucking fabulous!"

"No argument here; I've been listening to her since before you could walk."

"Whatever!"

Over time, Alexander, who started off as just a tryst, became a real friend. Like many before him, and quite a few since, out of the lonely angst of lustful craving emerged a confidant. Little else could have brought Alexander and many other, often enduring, gay friends to me over the years. Once in a while, some innocent straight person will ask, "How did you two become friends anyway?"

Do you really want to know?

It's funny to think back about a conversation that I had with Gary, this older gay man I met and befriended after we met at an adult bookstore. I was twenty-two years old at the time and still in the closet. He became a mentor to me as I listened to him try to forecast life after coming out. I told him that I was ready to be open about my gayness, that I wanted to stop meeting gay people only for sex, and that I wanted to have some "real" friends. Gary laughed and said, "You'll soon learn that gay people do not have friends. They only have ex-lovers."

It would take many years before I could see that he wasn't that far off.

8

More Was Better:
Sex with Friends

Chris Packard

I started having sex with guy friends when I was around thirteen—earlier if you count the sexual game playing during my preteens. With girl friends I experimented with sex in my late teens and early twenties, but always found nonsexual friendship more satisfying with them. Having sex with guys made a lot of sense to me because it was an extension of our friendship, a logical move when the line between "like" and "love" became blurred. Using playground logic, I believed that when it came to guys, sex signified the closest possible friendship, and I was prepared to have a lot of close friends. More was better, which to me meant more sex equaled more friends.

On overnights, after lights were out, often in bedrooms where dangerous bigger brothers lay sleeping, my best friends—a sequence of perhaps half a dozen same-age boys before I turned eighteen—and I would toss and turn, using the disguise of sleep to worm our way toward a pleasure we never spoke about. For hours the ruse kept us up: sleepless, restless, sighing, drifting, listening, tingling, and waiting for wordless responses in those otherwise dark and silent bedrooms. The next morning, tousled and pulpy, after a muted breakfast, we'd exchange a hasty flash of eyes and a muttered "see ya later" until the next time. Then, to my bedroom I went for furious-fisted solitary relief.

In another best friend's swimming pool, grappling underwater until explosions of laughter forced us up; or illustrating acrobatics on the trampoline; or demonstrating a wrestling pin; then, an afternoon of bendings, kneelings, and slurpings with my buddy in his bedroom seemed like the very definition of a good day. Sexual play at swim team camp, church camp, or in the locker rooms at school, reinforced the robust unity I felt with my close guy friends. We were boisterous boys, and if sex includes erotic play, then I had all sorts of sexual encounters with same-age friends throughout my childhood. Being the product of a middle-class family in Middle America, I suspect that my experiences are not unusual. While orgasms with my partners often eluded us until I was in college, I enjoyed kissing and groping and body exploring with most of my best friends and many more casual ones from all of my social groups: school, Youth for Christ, my neighborhood park, my swim team, my 4-H club, my Cub Scout Troop, and my YMCA Indian Guide group.

Everyday life for me, after the age of ten, was erotic, consciously so, in the broadest sense of the word, since every sensation that impressed itself upon my skin, or flooded my nose, or whispered in my ear, was new and, for that reason alone, thrilling. Denial of sensation and shame about indulging in prohibitions are powerful internal inhibitors, and I suffered their constraints later, in my twenties, but those didn't stop my yearnings nor my explorations. And I don't remember much chagrin about what seemed to me playful and inconsequential shenanigans. To me, the nighttime gropings were like dreams: illogical, fantastically incongruous, full of nonsequiturs, symbolically significant but undecipherable in daylight logic. I am not alone among those who were surprised by what were called, in the library books I read, "nocturnal emissions." Far from being ashamed of those wonderful orgasmic squirts that came from such fantastic dream-images, I enjoyed them but never in the daytime spoke about them. In the same way did I consider our wakeful nighttime adolescent sexual activity to be thoroughly pleasurable, but never in the daytime confessed.

I was fully aware of the changes my body went through as I grew from boy to man. Delayed puberty made me perhaps more intellectually aware than some of my friends, whose early development appeared as armpit hair before age ten, cracked voices at eleven, and moustaches by thirteen. My markers of manhood came slowly, and I felt left behind. Moodily I studied the bodies of my bigger, hairier, louder, rougher friends, dismayed by my skinnier, squeakier, neutered body. I have journal entries announcing the emergence of each of my first five pubic hairs not too many pages before reports of my first driving lesson. As a competitive swimmer, I raced against same-aged guys. What more pathetic sight is a race between a coltish late-bloomer and a sleek Apollo in Speedos diving off the starting blocks? Not only was I a late developer, but I was a slow learner in the school of sensations. Sex with friends remained a language of moles, earthworms, and other blind burrowers. Still, I managed to grow.

As my body finally woke up, so too did my mind expand. I started to resent the macho idiocies of my jock friends. We swimmers enjoyed a somewhat secure place in the ruthless social hierarchy of middle school swarms, but the cost of maintaining status among the casual cruelties of male locker room cultures was too high. In the jock world, I heard all the usual disparagements of fags and sissies. I also started to hear the hollow hypocrisy of that homophobic cruelty. At first, I thought the sex I was having with my buddies didn't fall into the category of what feminine boys did, and I believed my friends and I were exempt from the dreaded label. I didn't know what to call it, but our sex seemed robust and healthy, urgent, while feminine boys (and feminine girls, for that matter) seemed to be nonsexual, or their sexuality didn't fit with mine. I was happy to let the mystery of feminine sexuality remain a mystery, while I explored the more familiar sexuality of masculinity.

At about the time we all started driving, the sex I was having with friends took a spiritual turn. I quit the swim team and started smoking a lot of pot, grew my hair, started listening to Jefferson Airplane, Hendrix, and Uriah Heep. The Beatle's "Lucy in the Sky with Diamonds" made a lot of sense to me. I started reading Timothy Leary, Ram Das, and Carlos Castaneda. *Siddhartha* moved me profoundly, and I explored Zen Buddhism.

And I bonded even closer with my friends, assisted by psychedelic hallucinogens. We fancied ourselves a tribe, joined by what we thought was a profound relationship with other universes and a common interest in higher consciousness. We would drop acid and have parties while parents were away, or out on the bluffs overlooking the Kaw River. Our hedonistic tribalism lasted through the night and sometimes ended with dreamy couplings as the drugs wore off. Sex with friends on acid, in the late stages of tripping, I came to believe, is truly nirvana. Again the overnights, again the late-night sleepless "sleep," again the wordless owl-eyed departures in the morning. After a night of tripping came Fantasia-like kaleidoscopes of colors, traces, and sparks. Ear engorging mushrooms of sound emerged from the mere rustle of sheets. Intoxicating scents of teenage male arousal swam through my limbic system like wriggling tadpoles. For me the sensations provided tremendous insight, and in fact love, but not the kind of love that binds. We were friends, after all, still prone to casual "Later, dude" commitments and feigned indifference about our night-time rumpus.

That it was tremendously communicative but totally nonverbal sex, invited interpretation. Without language, without daytime mutual acknowledgement, I could define our sex any way I wanted, and I wanted to believe it was the language of spirits. I was reading Carl Jung at that time, and was beginning to understand that sex was both a symbol and an act. Long before I read Emerson and Whitman, and in his own warped way Thoreau, I was starting to believe that the human connection to the deities was through impulse, including the sexual or erotic. In a vague way this mysticism was tied up with nature and the male biological drive to seed every orifice that will permit him entrance. The sensual indulgences my friends and I practiced at night, long after girlfriends had been dropped off, compelled by wordless bodies yearning, seemed closer to divinity—to "nature"—than to any received creed or instructed sexuality. Like same-sex acolytes at altars that denied the gods of texts and institutions, my friends and I surrendered the social constraints of our daytime worlds and, assisted by recreational drugs, indulged wholly in instincts that were beyond language.

Skinny teenage drug-addled boys squirming on a couch, pretending to be asleep: to voyeurs and pornographers, this is a scene ripe for marketing, but from the perspective of one of the boys on that couch, the encounters were sublime. Our wordless communication seemed like the language of angels. Governed by a tissue-thin mutual denial of words, but relatively unconstrained in our physical actions, our senses guided us with a magnetic pull toward each other. Orgasm came to mean not the squirting of semen but a tantric hours-long elevation of consciousness through the physical senses that took place in another world. At least that's how I saw it.

Call me a purist, but I stopped doing drugs when the so-called designer hallucinogens were introduced: microdot, MDA, angel dust. I left Kansas for good, went to college on a scholarship and formalized the free love doctrines I'd been exploring in high school. I experimented freely, and so did those with whom I experimented. The difference between sex with friends in high school and sex with friends in college was that we talked about it. "Let's play," said Todd, as he climbed through my dormitory window, "but don't tell my girl-friend." In a sleeping bag out in the woods, David and I laughed and kissed and sucked and slurped and fucked our way through the night, then wrote poetry about it during the day. Marty, Caesar, and I got na-ked a few times every semester, shoved our mattresses together, lit candles and traded massages while talking about how masculinity prevented us from divulging our vulnerability.

Adjacent to the Antioch College campus is a thousand-acre nature preserve, where many a sylvan grotto hosted many an undergraduate's frolic. After Saturday night college dance parties featuring rock and roll gyrations, all sexual liaisons became known when pairs or three-somes showed up, tousled and sexed up, at the common cafeteria on Sunday mornings. Our showers and dormitories were strictly coed, and several times I explored playful sexuality while showering in groups.

At this same time I discovered a body of literature that celebrated male-male sexual expression within friendship structures that defied the narrow-minded American middle-class norm. What used to be wordless squirmings in high school I discovered were articulated in works of the world's greatest literature. From St. Augustine's deli-cious homoerotic parable about stealing pears to Plato's perverse ex-planation of love in *The Symposium,* I learned that experiments with words were like experiments with bodies: they teach, they uncover new possibilities, they stimulated the mind's nerves. Particularly in burlesque literature, lessons about the sex I was having with friends emerged in characters like Moll Flanders and Joseph Andrews, whose guilt-free sexual charlatanism got rewarded in novels that seemed revolutionary, for all their seventeenth century references. The erotic scenes in *Paradise Lost,* particularly between angels (so famously ungendered but still entirely Apollonian), grabbed my imagination and justified my own sense that sex with male friends induced human divinity. I snickered over D.H. Lawrence's impassioned screeds against Victorianism, but held my own fascination with the Gothic and ex-treme sexual imagery in *Jane Eyre, Middlemarch,* and *Jude, the Ob-scure.* The powerful engine of erotic discourses in novels and poetry floated stories and words on a sea of universal significance.

For all the sex I had in college, with people I called friends, and af-ter college when I had migrated to the male sexual culture of New

York City in the early 1980s, I promised sex to many more than those with whom I actually had it. I regret these empty or broken promises. I thought that casual sex was like casual friendship: no real obligation except mutual curiosity, governed by whim. Having sex first, or at least a kiss, became a way to start up a friendship, or provide the groundwork upon which a friendship could be built. The notion that permanent promises came with the kissing, the undressing, the hungry appreciation of aroused bodies, was ludicrous in my mind. Fidelity seemed a quaint idea that enforced an impossible, not to mention bourgeois, ideal.

Many were the arguments with girlfriends in my early twenties over the notion of sexual fidelity, while with guys the sexual encounter seemed predicated on a big "if." With David I never felt obliged, but often went back for more. Todd and I agreed that the magnet that drew us together was "just physical," and we maintained separate girlfriends on the side. Spooning with Marty or blowing Alain in the showers didn't seem to imply exclusivity. Walt Whitman had taught me by then that the rise and fall of arousal, like the sea, was as unceasing and as indiscriminate—almost impersonal. No connection except the felt one mattered, and feeling is nothing if not transitory. As the sun organizes the earth, yet appears to leave it regularly, so too did I organize my sexual friendships. I shined on all, and on each, but on none permanently.

I still hold to these principles, but I don't have sex with my friends anymore. Making myself sexually available to large numbers of people was tremendously taxing. It takes a lot of work to connect sexually with anyone, and practice doesn't ease the effort. The lessons, however, from decades of whimsical sexual indulgences are the basis for whatever wisdom I have acquired about friends and sex. I don't regret the promiscuity I practiced with friends, and I'm grateful for returning the interest. Before I turned forty I mistook that effort as sexual frisson, ever bubbling up like an eternal fountain of youth. But since then I've relinquished the effort.

I was not a pioneer in the sexual revolution, but I enjoyed the permissive philosophy that the revolutionaries created in the mass media in the 1970s and early 1980s. Drag queens and free love hippies founded a philosophy that permitted the kind of sexual exploring that I so enjoyed in my youth.

9

The Crossing

E. M. Kahn

I could tell Chris was scared, I could see it around his eyes, even through his thick eyeglass lenses. How easily we can read fear in another. How do we know this? Some remnant of our predatory instincts from hunting days on the savannahs? We know danger and we know fear in others. Of course, this trip was supposed to be fun, and here he was, at the helm of a thirty-foot sailboat crossing Buzzards Bay in twenty-five-knot winds with waves sloshing over our bow. There was something going on between us, something about sharing the thrill and danger of rough weather sailing.

Chris had been with me for three days now, since his arrival on a drizzly Friday morning at Woods Hole, Massachusetts. He came up by bus, although he was not to be found on the 9:30 a.m. express from Boston as he promised. I was disappointed, a little hurt, and went off for a slow breakfast alone with the *New York Times*.

But then he did show up, two hours later, looking tired and drained and pale from being awake most of the night traveling by train from New York to Boston then the bus connection down to Woods Hole. I was walking away from my boat, off for some sightseeing when, poof, there he was, sauntering down the alley leading to the marina. He looked sleepy and tousled and still cute.

"Well, there you are!"

"Un-huh."

"But you weren't on the other bus. Where did you come from? I was a little concerned." But really I was afraid that I would be alone another day.

On the Meaning of Friendship Between Gay Men

"Amtrak was screwed up getting to Boston. I caught the next bus."

"Okay. Well, then, hello there." I put my arms around him and felt him yield into my embrace. He felt nice this close, but I could sense his energy was way down. He was twenty-six, not quite half my age, and had a more delicate constitution, without great reserves of will and energy.

"I never really went to sleep last night anyway," he told me. "I was writing a story for a trashy online *zine*."

"Something raunchy?"

"Not really, kind of sad, about some mixed up guys, I'll tell you more later."

"You look tired. Do you want to eat? Or how about just come back to the boat, it's right there." My thirty-foot sailboat was in the very first slip, hardly fifty feet behind us.

It was nice that he was not the least embarrassed by our holding each other right there on the street. I liked that about him. He was free of all that uptightness more common to men of my own era, a caution built over years of being hurt or humiliated or even attacked.

I watched how he negotiated the little ballet of stepping from dock to boat, getting over the mess of crisscrossed mooring lines and the boat's own lifelines and stanchions. Yes, I liked him a lot, but still I watched with the narrowed eye of an old skipper sizing up a new crewman for signs of how he handled himself. After twenty years around boats I fancied I could spot a potential klutz right away, even if I did have romantic designs. The ship always came first. He grabbed the shrouds, shifted his weight onto the edge of the deck and carefully straddled over the lines and wires to step onto the foredeck. I opened the hatch for him to come below. Mercifully, he only had one knapsack. Clothes were not a big part of his traveling kit.

Chris had in fact been out with me once before on a very pleasant day sail on Long Island Sound. I was impressed then. Here was this academic type, small build, not especially pumped-up with muscles, a bit shy about even taking off his shirt to reveal a still rather boyish and soft torso, yet he was quick and confidant. He was genuinely smart and not intimidated by new things and situations. He was eager to learn and not afraid of the water that day.

Nor did the action of the boat that first time unsettle him: heeling over when going to windward, the boom slamming across during a tack or gybe, the fire drill of letting one jib sheet spin off its winch and then cranked in again on the opposite side of the boat. He had been on small boats but never a sailboat. He liked this. Chris seemed to welcome the challenge of understanding what was going on. I saw him as smart, yet not arrogant, and carried a confidence that said *I may not be big but I have brains and know how to use them.*

Barely half an hour on the water that first day and he noticed already that there was a very specific way I would wrap all the ropes around any of the cleats mounted to the deck of the boat. It was a common sailor's half hitch, the proper way to cleat a line, any line, so that it would never ever come off, yet in an urgent situation could be flipped off easily with two fingers, no matter how much strain might be on the working part of the rope. It was a method of fastening a line that I had trusted my own life to many times before, and Chris saw early on that there was some special purpose to this elegant way of crossing and tucking the line under itself. He wanted to learn it, and in minutes after I showed it to him in slow motion, he grasped it, and I was impressed. This was a basic bit of seamanship that has eluded more than 50 percent of other sailors I have known, regardless of years of experience.

"You really look wasted. You can stay on board and sleep, I'll come back for you in two hours. Is that okay?" I asked him, once we were down inside the dry cabin.

"Yeah, I hope you don't mind. Can I stretch out here?" he said, still standing in the middle of the cabin looking a bit lost. With his newness to me, he made the boat seem bigger.

"You can go forward into the V-berth. Do you want anything to drink? There's juice here in the cooler."

"Oh, this is fine right here," and he stretched himself out sleepily on the port side settee. I brought him a pillow from my bunk up forward. "You sure you're okay, alone for a while?" I was being formal and a good host. He was already easing into the acceleration lane to Dreamland.

I left him to rest and went to a slide show about the use of computer generated charts and integrated electronic navigational systems for super tankers transiting the waters of Prince William Sound, Alaska. Much to my surprise, there were nearly fifty others in the pitched lecture hall at the Woods Hole Oceanographic Institution. Chris remained asleep much of that rainy afternoon. I went to the aquarium after a long walk to Nobska lighthouse, overlooking Vineyard Sound and Martha's Vineyard. The day was grim, the winds strong and the seas rough and churned-up out there. I was not unhappy being here in port for a while.

My visitor came back to life about 3 p.m. Was it his youth or his delicateness? It was like he'd been transformed by the sleep while I was away. There was color in his face, a brightness to his brown eyes, a flush of revived energy about him. Would he sleep with me later that night? I wondered and hoped. How easily each time I had embraced him did he seem to merge into my arms and chest, how nice it had been to kiss him good-night the last time I had seen him, saying good-bye for a long time on 36th Street outside his jumbled loft.

I had only this one night to make this happen, since Frank would be arriving the next afternoon from Provincetown accompanied by Dian. On the surface Frank and I were supposed to be boyfriends, but it was a very open relationship. My original itinerary was already pretty screwed up, and I was calling people every night to tell them where to meet me since I decided not to bother trying to sail into small craft warnings through Buzzards Bay and Cape Cod Bay. Getting up to P-Town and then Boston and Plymouth seemed crazy now. So I left word at Frank's guesthouse where to find me in Woods Hole. Sunday we would all leave aboard *BEVEL* together and sail across Buzzards Bay to New Bedford where Chris could catch another bus home.

The marine forecast that Friday night was dreadful: northwest winds twenty-five to thirty-five knots with gusts to forty, seas six feet and more on the bays. I certainly was not going to drag Chris out into that, nor did I have the stomach to put myself through such an ordeal just to get to Provincetown merely to keep to my elaborate schedule, which I had printed and circulated to all the crew. It showed daily mileages, anticipated times of arrival and departure all in twenty-four-hour, or military, time. Very efficient. But that had been an exercise in logistical planning for the sheer challenge of it. The trip was supposed to be fun, and I had already begun this two-week summer sailing vacation with an exhausting and anxious twenty-two-hour overnight passage from my home port of City Island to Block Island.

I told Chris the next morning that we would stay here instead of bashing about in six-foot seas and asked if he was disappointed we weren't sailing.

"No, no. That's fine. I'm happy just being up here. I have no set plans."

I thought guests on board my sailboat were entitled to at least some real sailing rather than spending several days in a cramped cabin tied to a dock. We went for a walk early Saturday around the Eel Pond, I wanted to show Chris some of the handsome old colonial homes that gave Woods Hole its character. But really, I wanted to see for myself what Buzzards Bay looked like. From the same beach I had gone swimming with all the local kids two days earlier, the seas were whipped up into a white and angry froth. Yes, my boat could handle this, and once out into the Bay we'd have the wind basically behind us making for an exhilarating and fast trip. I didn't tell Chris this.

"Well, what about we switch to Plan B?" I asked.

"What was that?" Chris asked, trying to remember if we really had talked about that.

"We'll go to the Gay Pride Parade in Hyannisport, it's today at eleven a.m., let's check the poster I saw last night. We just have to figure out how to get there. Actually, I'm a Kennedy groupie and I've always wanted to see where they lived and all that."

Again the sparkle in his eyes. This was a small and handsome and manly-looking young face, with a nicely shaped jaw and an appealing bit of male stubble around his chin. I was attracted especially by this token bit of showing off his wee bit of beard since it had the effect of emphasizing his boyishness even more. The wire-rimmed glasses gave him a slightly owlish look, with his eyes wrinkled and deep set, so that he seemed vulnerable, and thus maybe more available to me. I was eager for some insight into who he was, some way that would rush along that elusive process of getting to know someone. Hoping of course that he would come to like me, that some kind of magical bonding would happen between us.

"How are you doing up there?" I asked Chris from the companionway over the noise of the wind and sloshing waves. He was at the wheel steering for me, steering for all of us. I needed him now. I needed someone steady and reliable to handle the helm so that I could navigate and look after important details around the boat.

"Oh yeah. I'm fine. What's our course supposed to be? I'm doing about 275 or 280." *BEVEL* lurched forward, the bow rose up sharply and I tensed myself, and watched Chris at the helm. Normally, my instincts would be to look forward and see what kind of wave we were about to slam into. But for a moment I was more curious to see what *he* would do, how this novice would deal with a rogue wave. I had never really told him much about handling steep waves. Yet almost as if plugged into my own feel for the boat, he brought the bow up with a sharp turn of the wheel so that we took the worst of the curling seas not quite square on the bow but rather about five to ten degrees off the bow, where she could ride easily up and over, and not come to a dead stop from the force of the water. Chris had the feel of it. It was part of being afraid. We were both afraid that Sunday morning heading out of Woods Hole and trying to cross Buzzards Bay. Right away, we knew without talking that we needed each other.

Frank had been through some choppy and windy conditions with me before. But today with his head full of Dramamine and his digestion in the grip of a demon, he was wedged into a corner of the cockpit, trying to focus on the horizon as we hobbyhorsed and slammed around. Dian was flat on his back trying to stay out of the way on the starboard side of the cockpit, looking pale despite his Latino complexion. With his eyes closed he kept apologizing for not being more helpful. No one dared go below except me, and only to study the chart and figure out how far off course for New Bedford the current was setting us.

"Listen, if you can do 275 we're in pretty good shape to get across. Do you want something to drink?"

Crash. Chris ducked to one side as a plume of spray from a wave flew over his head. Frank didn't even know about it. Dian gripped the stainless steel guardrails harder. I came back up into the cockpit. I was getting all bruised trying to hang onto things down below at the chart table. Chris, not usually very talkative, looked tense with concentration.

"Would you like me to clean off your glasses?" I asked him, leaning against the compass directly in front of him. It took him a moment to understand what and why I was asking such a thing. His lenses were caked with salt spray.

"Oh yes, that would be very helpful," he answered, with a note of surprise at such a gracious offer. He pried off the thin wire frames from his ears carefully with one hand, kind of twisting his head away, and I took them from him and ducked back down below to the galley sink to run some clean water on them. The first time I had seen him take off his glasses, a calm afternoon during a lunch break on the boat a month ago, he didn't look as helpless as I had expected. In fact, he suddenly looked kind of mean, sturdy and a bit unpredictable, with his eyes narrow and squinty. At the wheel now he couldn't read the compass two feet in front of him and just kept the boat moving through the wind shifts and sloppy seas by feel. I took a clean tissue and carefully dried off his lenses.

"Ah, that's wonderful," his eyes looked sharp and alert now through the clean glass discs, after he replaced them. I could hear a slightly nervous quiver in his voice, a dry-mouthed formality to his sentences as he tried to mask his fear while handling a 10,000-pound sailboat in rougher conditions than he had ever imagined he would sail in.

"Well, it is a good deal better than yesterday," I shared with him in a professional matter-of-fact way. I stood close by him, just in front of the compass, staying there to give him assurance, though never touching the wheel, letting him know that I had no intention of suddenly grabbing the wheel myself and thereby robbing his sense of controlling the boat.

"This is about as high as we can sail on this course, though it is about twenty-five to thirty degrees off our rhumb line to New Bedford." I spoke close to his ear, the skipper conferring with his number two. "All you have to do is try to keep her moving well, you know, watch the *woolies* on the front edge of the jib up there. We'll cross the Bay on this tack then tack over to starboard to find the entrance to New Bedford."

I know he didn't completely understand the strategy, but that didn't matter so much. He did know from just that first sail earlier on the Sound the very basics about keeping the sails full and drawing and working a boat upwind by keeping a watch on the red wool streamers sewn along the leading edges of both sails. He had grasped that they showed how the wind flowed across both sides of the sail, and thus how to maximize the power from the wind as it bent around both main and jib and allowed us to perform the miracle of modern yachting: effectively sailing upwind and thus cheating nature.

"Oh Gene, I think I might be sick soon. Should I go over the side or do you want me to use the toilet down below?" It was Dian, perking up finally. I hoped not to have to deal with really sick passengers on what was actually a very exhilarating passage this morning. I told him to feel free to use the ocean as he needed and he slipped his head over the edge of the deck. I felt sorry for him, and worried if the sight or smell might get to me. Instead I brought him up some fresh water. "Oh, you're just too kind, my captain." Well, he might be seasick, I thought, but he could still camp. That was a good sign.

The second time he threw up over the rail, he actually looked better afterwards. Some people were like that. Once the terror and the tension went through them they were stable. Color and a tentative smile returned to his darkish face. With the sunglasses and light colored khakis he looked like he was on board a cruise ship waiting for the cabin steward.

"You know, this is really beautiful out here, just kind of bouncy, but I'm glad you asked me along."

"Here, try nibbling on some dry bread, just to keep something inside your stomach," I told him, and handed him a few Saltines. He was definitely perking up.

"Do you ever get sick?" He looked at me through his sunglasses, curious and maybe a bit envious.

"Well, I have gotten nauseous at times, but I've never had to throw up," I granted.

I looked back at Chris, who tilted his head a bit closer to me saying, "I just have too much of a sense of control to even let myself get sick."

"Yes, I know the type," I told him quietly. "You're like me."

We were well clear of Woods Hole. The wind was blowing from the northwest about twenty to twenty-five knots with some stronger gusts. The boat was a little overpowered and I needed to reduce some sail. It should only take about three-and-one-half hours to reach New Bedford, but I wanted to keep the boat under easy control out there. I moved back toward Chris and began to explain how I would lower part of the mainsail and would need him, or someone, to ease off the mainsheet for a while once I climbed onto the top of the cabin to reach the boom and tie down some of the mainsail. He would have to keep us moving along for a few minutes with just the jib drawing. The day was clear and sunny, and all the features across the shore six miles away were sharp on the horizon. This was scary, but nothing like the hair-raising sail in dense fog heading at top speed into the cliffs of Block Island the previous week. The day might have been windy, but it was also glorious sailing.

That first night he arrived, the two of us cooked a simple dinner on board: spaghetti and a salad. It was late and still raining and we didn't want to go out. Afterwards, while he was reading, I made up the bed in the V-berth where I normally sleep up in the bow. I told him there was plenty of room for both of us up there, or I could set up another bed for him in the main cabin, if he preferred. He seemed to acquiesce easily. I wanted his company—a lot. I wanted to pull him on top of me and taste the inside of his mouth and feel the pulsing behind his closed eyes against my lips. I didn't care so much what kind of sex we had or not, only to bring him into that comforting intimacy of sharing a bed together and then finding him still there again in the morning, next to me. I didn't exactly miss Frank's companionship, since he was not easy to sleep next to anyway, but I felt an aching for touch and warmth.

Instead Chris stayed up reading and listening to music in the main cabin. Growing tired, I went forward and I lay there tense with expectations until I finally drifted off. About 1 a.m. or so, I woke up and was still alone. Apparently, he didn't take up my invitation. That was his choice, I told myself. Then I realized he was sleeping without any pillows or bedding and I slipped out of the V-berth to give him sheets and stuff. The reading light was still on above him but Chris was asleep again in his clothes on the settee berth, with just a Mexican blanket under his head, his book and eyeglasses lying on the table next to him. I guess I couldn't orchestrate everything quite so perfectly, I thought, and went back to sleep. In the morning I remembered what his loft in the city looked like and realized he was used to sleeping under pretty *ad hoc* circumstances. He was easy to please.

The next day we made our way to Hyannisport and caught up with the Gay Pride Parade, walking along on the sidewalk. It was a pretty small group, just doing a big square around the center of town with a friendly police escort and curious homeowners on their front lawns waving. We stepped off the curb, sped up past all the women's banners and slipped back in among some nicely dressed college-age men. Now we were in the parade. Together. Afterwards we wandered among all the booths on the town green and then went off for lunch where we wound up talking about theater and rock music. We were over twenty years apart in age yet shared an uncanny affinity for the same music.

We returned by town bus to Woods Hole at the end of the day and found Frank and Dian already on board the boat. My private time with Chris was over.

"It's up to you, you're the skipper," Frank told me as we all began to move toward bedtime later that same day. The fantasy of Frank finding romance with Dian and me finding passion with young Chris was slipping away for this chapter. It was my role to assign bunks, exercise authority and wisdom. All that night at dinner I was nervous, not about the sleeping arrangements, but about the crossing the following morning. I knew what none of the others knew: that it was going to be very rough, and that we had to leave really early, 6:30 a.m. in fact. No leisurely breakfasts and a stroll around the picturesque town. After three days I wanted to get moving, and we had to time our departure with the openings of the drawbridge that closed in the Eel Pond.

Frank and I, as usual, shared the V-berth. Chris stayed in the main cabin settee and Dian was given the quarter berth, just aft of the nav station on the same port side. Up forward, in the dark, I felt Frank press against me, and soon felt his cock stiffen reliably. Very soon we were fucking, drawn again by our mutual needs. It happened so easily. We had so many differences, certainly, but we did fit together here so wonderfully. I kicked aside the covers. Frank kept trying to "shush" me each time I exhaled with a gasp of overwhelming pleasure. He clasped his hand over my mouth to quiet me, making it hard to breath, but also dominating me, and that made it all even more arousing. This time we came together and that was so good. After a few minutes of quiet I crawled out of the V-berth to use the head, and heard our two "boys" earnestly chatting away like young campers. Chris and Dian, sharing baseball cards by flashlight under their covers.

For the third time Frank asked me if anything had "happened" between me and Chris. No, I wanted to tell him candidly, it's just you and me for the long haul. We fell asleep very quickly.

"This has got to be Mattapoisett Bay we're sailing into," I called back from my perch against the mast. "We're miles and miles up north. We have to tack back down the Bay until we find the buoys leading into New Bedford." The crossing under sail had taken us far upstream of our destination, as I expected, but it was still a much easier ride than if we had tried to motor directly into the wind and seas, which would have been exhausting. By now we were already on the north coast of Buzzards Bay, and while the wind was still strong, the seas had settled down a lot. I couldn't identify a single buoy nearby but knew we had to run west along the coast.

Frank, now feeling better, showed Dian how to handle the jib and main sheets as we changed tacks. Everyone was up and useful. For a while I got frantic trying to identify a rocky point that was marked with only a few buoys. There were rocks all around a spit of land that lay right on our course, so we bore away again toward the middle of the bay, losing some of the ground upwind we had earlier worked to gain. Better to sail another twenty minutes than run up on poorly marked rocks. Finally the long string of red and green buoys marking the entrance channel into New Bedford came into view.

Chris looked peaked out but happy and I asked Frank if he cared now to take the helm. He was glad for a chance to be busy and useful once again. A line of red buoys began to arrange themselves off our starboard side like the lights of a runway. We could now see clearly the opening into the inner harbor, through the hurricane barrier. Red to the right, green on the left coming in from the sea. So easy.

Dian was starting to sing and camp again, in full form. I put my hands on both hips, cocked my head and said, "Well, listen to *her*! Miss Salty Dog's back from the dead."

"Oh girl, don't you know it. Where are my dancing shoes?"

"Are these your little pumps with all that nasty throw-up all over them," I asked politely, grabbing Dian's hairy ankles.

He giggled uncontrollably. "You're bad, you're just bad," was all he could reply this time.

Chris went below, now that things were calmer, and I showed him the chart. He bent close as I traced our course across the Bay and how we wound up so far north, and the dangerous point we had to get around to avoid a two-foot spot. He studied the line of buoys leading into the harbor, starting to appreciate the Coast Guard's logic to help mariners find their way. It was something else he seemed eager to understand and learn. I knew he could if he wanted to. I also knew that something important had happened between us, something other than what I had expected.

I had played out for him a special role. Rather than fiddle with him as a plaything, with all the attending delights and risks, we had found another space to play within. He had plenty of boyfriends, but what he longed for was a mentor, an older man who knew things, serious things that were not abstractions, things that had the unforgiving and dangerous thud of nonacademic reality, things that took courage and nerve, though not necessarily strength. It was that dynamic of being trusted and knowing that this trust was more important than anything else in the world, that failing was not an option, and that the circumstances of this trust had to be really scary, made it all the more intoxicating. So I failed at all the coy steps to con this young man out of his clothes. Instead in effect I said to him, *I need you now. I trust you even if you don't think you can do this. And of course, along with this, you already know that I love you.*

10

The Country Club

Michael E. Thomas II

Friendships are like ideas. They come, they go, rising and falling, side by side. You get a new idea, you spend time and energy thinking about it, you adapt to it. Then it may start to wane or even die altogether.

Back in the late 1980s, as a young Republican at my conservative Christian college, I explored the ideas of sixteenth century reformer John Calvin. Within a few months of resisting the principles of Calvinism, I eventually took to them. I became a Calvinist: I had Calvinist friends, took Calvinist outings, and engaged in Calvinist-centered conversations. Calvin taught that all humans were naturally immoral, that only a chosen few were loved by God, and that every single detail in the universe was predestined by God. I daily consumed the dense and voluminous writings of John Calvin like a kid eating candy. A few years later, I had a long-distance phone conversation with one of my closest former Calvinist buddies to tell him that I was now gay and about to vote for the Democratic Candidate for President: Bill Clinton. His long silence and eventual reply stunned me.

He said, "I only have one question for you: In your new belief system, is Jesus still the Christ?"

I said, "For the Christian Believer, yes."

We never spoke again.

That was hard. Ours was a friendship I would have loved to keep, even though it died with the death of my belief in Calvinism specifically; religion in general. I almost wished that I could have forced myself to be a believer just so I could have kept that friendship. But I couldn't, so I didn't.

On the Meaning of Friendship Between Gay Men

Because of this experience, and many more like it, I saw how friendship plays a part in authenticating our beliefs. When our friends share and reinforce our notions, it helps to make them feel real. Through friendship, we get to experience ourselves in whatever identity expresses who we best are. Since my early evangelical days, I've been exposed to many exciting ideas—and parallel friendships—that came and went. I'm now at least used to the whole process. I almost accept it. But still, there are a few ideas—and friendships—no matter how doomed, you really wish you could hold on to forever. I felt that way about my best gay friend, Gustavo Werner.

As a teenager, long before I met him, I hid my feelings for other men. Beneath the dark, secret confines, amid the highway truck stops and mall bathroom stalls, my gay feelings—and gay friendships—were a painful secret. But by the time I had met Gustavo, those feelings and those friendships blossomed in the wide-open spaces of New York City's gay life. Whereas being gay once felt shameful and made me miserable, it was now almost exclusively about pleasure and fun!

Gustavo and I met in the spring of 1997 at a New York City bathhouse in the heart of Chelsea called the West Side Club. He was gorgeous: a tall, dark haired, fair skinned, twenty-seven-year-old Argentinean with a hot dancer's ass. You could not walk by him without staring. This was exactly what I did as he strutted his stuff in front of me that first time wearing nothing but a snug-fitting white towel. He looked at me and said, "Hot," then vanished, for the moment anyway.

Looking back on this, I still cannot explain why we didn't have sex. After all, wasn't that why we were there? Clearly, Gustavo was my type and I was his. Yet, at that moment, perhaps we sensed that the potential for friendship trumped sex. We exchanged numbers later that night and quickly connected after that. He began to call me everyday at work. We saw each other three or four nights a week, sharing one of our favorite pastimes—going to the West Side Club. We would always leave together and talk and laugh about everybody there. I started to call him Stavito. He told me that his mother and I were the only two people who ever called him by that name, which was fitting since I was now his best friend. I liked that.

Stavito and I became inseparable. He renamed our favorite hangout The Country Club because, he said, in the Age of Giuliani, it was the only fun place left for gay men to go. He and I turned it into *our* country club. Since we were regulars, we recognized all the other regulars, even coming up with nicknames for them: "Avid Reader," "24/7," "Friday Night," "The Horny Priest," "The Hustling Hasid," and "Mi Vida n Amor." Stavito even came up with a nickname for me. Because I always had a book to read while I waited in line, he called me Leo Tolstoy, which I loved since, little did he know, Tolstoy was, and always will be, one of my favorite authors.

When we first met, Stavito said he loved how formal I was in my everyday speech and that I was the only person he knew who used phrases like "in general," "however," "insofar as," "inasmuch," "hitherto," and "heretofore." His favorite was "in general." He would run up to me on the street, screaming and laughing, then he'd give me a big kiss, snap his fingers, and say, "In general!"

I told him all about my sexual conquests, making sure to offer every detail, including the size of the guy's dick and the shape of his ass. Our expression for a guy with a flat butt was: "It's like a table, honey." I told him how much money I made; I told him my fears, my worries, my dreams; and I told him all about my family. I used to sleep over his apartment a lot on weekends and he and I would snuggle all night long. But, strangely enough, we never had sex. He used to cook me breakfast on Saturday mornings, and he would jump up and down like a little kid while watching his favorite cartoon, "Pinky and the Brain."

For some reason, which I can't recall, I gave Stavito a warning one night after we left The Country Club. I said, "Honey, listen, make sure you are careful in this place. A lot of these guys like to fuck raw. Don't you dare let them slip it inside you without a condom! We've got to be careful and look out for each other." He said, "I know what you mean, girl. And you know they'd love to get inside this booty!" I said, "I know."

One night after I arrived at his Upper West Side apartment for a big party he was hosting, I asked, "Where is Gustavo?" Someone said, "He's in his room in a K-hole. He can't respond to anyone until it wears off." I thought, "Oh, if anyone, he'll respond to *me*." I walked into his bedroom to see him looking a mess, sitting there with his head in the palm of his hands, like Rodin's famous *Thinker*. I kissed him gently on the cheek and whispered as sinisterly as I could, "Uh huh, honey, in general!" Laughter. Tears. Paralysis broken.

Stavito was so amusing. When he called and got my voicemail, he would always leave the longest, funniest messages. So I started to save them. To this day, I still have dozens. We had a fast, full, and fabulous friendship for about two years.

After that, things started to sour between us. It began when a mutual friend of ours questioned my relationship with Stavito. He used to describe us as frivolous and said that it held me back from any important growth and achievement. Not long after, I found myself feeling a little silly about our conversations—calling each other "girlfriend" all the time, him screaming "in general," calling me Leo Tolstoy. It was fun, but it was beginning to get stale. I started to grow weary always talking about this cute boy and that hot guy. I started to think differently about our time at The Country Club. Going there started to feel more like an addiction. I would go alone, without telling him, usually when I felt anxious and in need of some escape. I started to wonder how long I would put all my energy into anonymous sex, gay bars and clubs, late weekend nights, and circuit parties. I started to become easily annoyed by Stavito. All this developed slowly, as our once perfect friendship quietly, inevitably, slipped away. Without admitting it openly and directly, we drifted apart.

I called him one night and told him off on his answering machine. I ranted that our friendship seemed one-sided, that he was selfish, and that he just used me for favors. On and on I went. He returned my call and left a sweet, controlled message maintaining my right to express such a thing, but politely disagreeing.

Several months passed without any contact. Then we unexpectedly bumped into each other on Fire Island. The look on his face seemed to reflect my own feelings—concern, hurt, but relief in seeing each other. We slowly approached one another and fell into a gentle embrace.

I whispered, "Stavito, I'm so glad to see you. You look so good, honey."

He whispered back, "You do too, sweetheart."

"I've missed you so much, Stavito."

"Really?"

"Yes."

And I had. He looked different, even better than before. He had let the front of his hair grow long, swooping across his otherwise neatly cropped haircut. The saddest part of this meeting was, although this hug and these words were a blessing in the sense that it confirmed our past, we somehow recognized the impossibility of a future.

That was the last time we saw each other. After that, Stavito relocated to Miami. He found a boyfriend and began working as a flight attendant. I, too, found a boyfriend, and eventually lost touch with him for about a year. I moved on. My boyfriend Mark sometimes asked if I missed my old friend. I would shrug my shoulders and say, "Nah."

Mark and I started to redefine ourselves and our sexuality. Old ideas were replaced by new ones. We practiced an open relationship. We were no longer gay, but bisexual. To me, being bisexual meant more than just having sex with women. It meant that I was somehow a broader person, not shut in a box. We stopped celebrating holidays, considering it a waste of energy and too much obligation buying all those gifts. On Christmas, we would just go to the movies. We avoided socializing with our gay friends and made a point of seeing our straight friends. We hung out with swinging bisexual people. I could not believe my new life, like the time we had a tryst with a heterosexual couple, and being in bed with this beautiful Italian woman whom I had just met. She and I lay naked, snuggling, as we watched our boyfriends go at each other.

She said to me, "Look at him. He loves it."

I replied, "I know."

There were other new ideas and friendships. Mark and I participated heavily in the Ayn Rand philosophy group known as Objectivism. Instead of going to gay bars and clubs on Saturday nights, we went to a regular salon with a roomful of straight nerds who just could not get enough of Ayn Rand's ideas. I loved it.

After about a year of this, Mark and I decided to revisit our gay subculture. We took a brief weekend summer trip to the beaches of Fire Island. While there, I bumped into an old friend, Stavito's ex-roommate. I ran up to him like a happy puppy.

I said, "Hey, Scott! So how is our crazy Argentinean friend? Have you heard from him lately?" The look on his face told me everything.

"You don't know? He died a couple weeks ago. He had AIDS. Apparently, he picked up a bad parasite on a recent trip to South America and just couldn't shake it."

I froze. I couldn't grasp the information. Several thoughts occurred at once: Did he have AIDS all along? How can he be dead so quickly?

People don't die of AIDS like that any more. Was it a car accident? Something else? I tried to recall Stavito: his voice, his scent, his laughter like gurgling burps that ended with a crescendo into an effeminate howl. I tried to recollect our past as one ineffable whole.

I kept replaying the question that Stavito's old roommate asked me, "You don't know?" No, of course I didn't know. I didn't know because Gustavo didn't tell me. Again and again, I went over the reasons why I *should* have known.

Death can cause such rude awakenings. It draws a sharp separating stake between fantasy and reality. Hearing that he was gone seemed to jam the circuits in my head, where ideas and friendships merged, floated around, came and went, according to my own imagination. It seemed easy enough for me to think of friendships as flexible and as indispensable as my ability to form an idea around it. In this sense, friendships were indeed always coming and going. But Gustavo's death, this was something different for me. The inflexibility of it, the finality of it shocked me.

It would be many years before I understood that my relationship with Gustavo was really my relationship with a fantasy—not a real person. The fantasy was that Gustavo was perfect and our friendship was perfect. Being together meant there were no worries about being gay; that there was nothing to be ashamed about. There was no need for me to fear social ridicule, since I had Gustavo and he had me. Together we had fun, pleasure, escape from any and all of the concerns of gay life that might otherwise have weighed us down. The anxiety that I remembered from my closeted days seemed to dissolve during those blissful encounters with Gustavo. He gave me the protection I needed but couldn't give to myself, so much so that I could hardly see who he really was. Reality became a blur. We were hot for each other, but just never wanted to have sex. That was convenient. It kept me from ever asking *and* perhaps would have made the relationship too real. In my head, we had no secrets. We told each other everything. At the time, I thought we drifted apart for no apparent reason, like an outmoded idea. Perhaps when I stopped needing as much protection, I stopped needing him. I don't know. I'm still trying to figure it all out.

Dear Stavito: I wonder how things might have been different if I had seen *you,* and myself, apart from my imposed ideas and fantasies.

Just one last thing: Stavito, the West Side Club was *not* a country club. It was—plain and simple—a sex club and we just couldn't help ourselves from going there now could we? Might you still be here if we had?

PART V:
ON FRIENDSHIP AND SPIRITUALITY

– 11 –

Soul Friend

Thomas Lawrence Long

Here we are, you and I, and I hope a third, Christ, in our midst.

Aelred of Rievaulx

My friend, Ken, and I stand in the sanctuary of the abandoned English Cistercian Abbey of Rievaulx, "bare ruined choirs where late the sweet birds sang" as William Shakespeare might have imagined it. Hidden at the base of a steep hill beside "Rye Valley" because cleanliness was next to godliness for austere Cistercian monks in the twelfth century and off the beaten track because Cistercians love isolation, this once-thriving religious establishment was literally pulled down during the reign of the insatiably heterosexual Henry VIII, along with all the other monasteries and convents in England, who excused the desecration as a purging of vice—chiefly sodomy, he claimed—which he had also legislated into a capital crime, punishable by death. If ghosts haunt this place, they may include those of a sixteenth-century workman accidentally buried under a pile of rubble while razing

On the Meaning of Friendship Between Gay Men

the walls (but not discovered until archeological excavations in the nineteenth century), its last monks at the dissolution, and the medieval abbot whose writing about male friendship has made him a patron saint of queer men, Aelred of Rievaulx.

In a sermon glossing the biblical account of David and Jonathan, Aelred wrote:

> But in his great love, this young man kept faith with his friend. He was steadfast in the face of threats, unmoved by insults; forgetting renown, he thought only of service. He spurned a kingdom for the sake of friendship. This is what truly perfect, stable and lasting friendship is, a tie that envy cannot spoil, nor suspicion weaken, nor ambition destroy. A friendship so tempted yielded not an inch, was buffeted but did not collapse. In the face of so many insults, it remained unshaken. Go, therefore, and do likewise.

My goal in this essay—equal parts tribute and reflection—is to explore a tradition of soulful friendship between men, a tradition that is overtly homosocial if not explicitly homosexual, and to celebrate its incarnation in one friendship. This tradition has often been withheld by religious institutions from gay men and has usually been forgotten by gay men in their tendency to eroticize male relationships. Soul friendship, in contrast, denies neither the body nor the spirit.

If I have come to Yorkshire, ostensibly, to present a paper at the International Medieval Studies Congress at the University of Leeds, Ken is here because he wants to be with me. Earlier in the year when I described to him my planned summer itinerary in England, he said, "I would love to see some of England with you." Such is the way of friendship that a friend does not need to fish for an invitation; the friend speaks his heart.

This is my third visit to England in slightly over a decade, but Ken's first, and his journey is in some ways very much farther than mine. The only member of his immediate family to escape the limitations of life on an Indian reservation in landlocked Montana, Ken joined the Navy, which eventually landed him in Norfolk, Virginia, where he stayed. I came to Norfolk in 1984 at the direction of the Catholic bishop of Richmond, Virginia, to serve as associate pastor of a parish. Ken works as a database specialist for a pension fund; I, now a professor of English, writer and editor.

Shortly after I arrived in Norfolk, Ken and I met through the mediation of a friend named Bill Vesey, since passed into the communion of saints, who wanted to make sure that I had gay friends in Norfolk. I had only been ordained a few years and had already served as an intern in two parishes and as an associate pastor in a third. Bill prevailed upon his friend, Jack Jacknik, also since passed away, to invite me to his home for dessert, where I met Ken and other leadership of the Norfolk metro area's then-thriving Dignity chapter, a branch of an international support, education, and advocacy group for queer Catholics. I remember three things about that evening. First, I was insatiably thirsty because my rectory's cook had over-salted a chicken and rice dinner that I had suggested she make. (What a spoiled and pampered life a priest can live.) Second, my host and his guests and I were on cautiously good behavior. (How far could I trust these people, I wondered about them, and what is *his* story, they wondered about me.) And third, Ken was serenely quiet. In the manner of gay men with an honored guest of uncertain sexuality, several of the company that night preened and probed while I was bland and evasive. The mystique of priesthood has its charms, effecting both social and erotic capital. Ken was simply present, attentive.

For Aelred, a friend is "another self to whom you can speak on equal terms, to whom you can confess your failings, to whom you can make known your progress without blushing, one to whom you can entrust all the secrets of your heart." The trust on which this disclosure is based usually relies on quiet attendance, much as one tames a skittish animal. Neither trust nor the friendship that follows it can be imposed, which is why I am often guarded when someone announces, too hastily, "I think we're going to be close friends."

After I became involved with the Dignity chapter and became its chaplain, Ken and I had numerous occasions in each other's presence; frequently I was the guest at his home. Although Ken is in many respects an introvert, his unaffected and unpretentious hospitality betrays his generous capacity for friendship, and so the depth of his humanity. As Aelred wrote, "Those who have no friends are to be compared to beasts for they have no one with whom to rejoice, no one to whom they can unburden their hearts, or with whom to share their inspirations and illuminations." Whether it is in the artfully presented dish Ken brings to a potluck supper, or the preparation of tea and cake when a friend drops by on the spur of the moment, or the social event that he plans, there is both an agapic and erotic inflection to his friendship: donating himself and extending himself outward. For a quiet man, Ken has a wide and varied circle of friends.

Freely borrowing ideas from the Roman Cicero in *De Amicitia,* about which Aelred knew either from his aristocratic training or monkish learning, Aelred viewed friendship as "agreement on all things sacred and profane, accompanied by good will and love," which is as near as any to a universal definition, though they are more particularly the desiderata of spiritual friendship, of the soul friend. Not long after we became friends, Ken asked me to serve as his sponsor at confirmation. Although a lifelong Catholic, he had never been confirmed in adolescence. I was touched that he asked, particularly since the role of godfather at baptism or of sponsor at confirmation confers an intimacy that Canon Law recognizes as an impediment to marriage. According to Aelred, "Friendship is a stage bordering upon that perfection which consists in the love and knowledge of God, so that human beings from the experience of human friendship become friends of God." Even though we are both no longer involved in formal religious practice—having decided that Church membership is akin to an abusive marriage—there remains a spiritual registration to our friendship by which I recognize in Ken the theological virtues of faith, hope, and love.

Friendship, moreover, is forged in the crucible of hardship. If gay men celebrate the Body Electric, gay men of a certain age have also endured the body's rebellions. Ken and I came to confront HIV infection and AIDS in many of our friends during the 1980s and early 1990s, including our mutual friend Jack Jacknik, for whom Ken served as caretaker and, ultimately, executor. He and I have also sat by each other through our own illnesses. Our bodies, like those of most men at mid-life, have rebelled against the dreamy illusions of youth. "No medicine," according to Aelred, "is more valuable, none more efficacious, none better suited to the cure of all our temporal ills than a friend to whom we may turn for consolation in time of trouble—and with whom we may share our happiness in time of joy." Through two of his surgeries or my own episode of depression and of a vestibular disorder, Ken and I have kept each other company.

It is perhaps Ken's capacity for soulful hospitality that is most affecting. For some hosts, guests are an audience of a self-promoting spectacle, or frankly a nuisance. Ken simply makes room. In a treatise on charity, Aelred noted the need for the heart to be enlarged, "so as to become a great hospice in which to welcome all those who need our sympathy when they are sorrowful, or who would have us rejoice with them when they are glad." On two occasions, I have lived with Ken for extended periods of time, first when I left the priesthood, and second when I was between having sold one house and looking for another. He has done the same for many of his friends. Now he is doing so for his niece's son, who was about to become homeless. I admire, but cannot claim to approach, his generosity of spirit.

Soul friendship does not require explicit affiliation with a religious community or ideology. Perhaps that is the third person, the Christ, incarnated in our friendship, as Aelred states in the quotation that serves as an epigraph to this essay. Although Ken and I both no longer practice the Roman Catholic life, it is nonetheless the divinity of friendship that still binds us, the sanctifying power of *caritas* to make the heart more spacious and more forgiving. A benign ghost of that religion hovers around us like the spirit of Aelred in the ruins of Rievaulx Abbey.

REFERENCES

The mirror of charity: The speculum caritatis of St. Aelred of Rievaulx (1962). Translated and arranged by G. Webb & A. Walker. London: A. R. Mowbray.

"Spiritual friendship" (1983). Mary Eugenia Laker, trans. *The love of god, and spiritual friendship: Bernard of Clairvaux.* Abridged, edited, and introduced by J. M. Houston. Portland, OR: Multnomah Press.

PART VI:
ON FRIENDSHIP AND BEING ALONE

– 12 –

A String Theory of Friendship

Jay Quinn

To come up with a coherent, thoughtful discussion of friendship proved to be more difficult than I imagined. For me, contemplating the constellation of people in my life whom I could describe as friends was as difficult to explain as the infinity of space or the sub-quark level of existence. People are simultaneously simple and complex and what makes them attractive or interesting to me is as nearly inexplicable. Friends simply are. They exist as anomalies in the course of all of my human reactions. To think about why some people are differentiated as friends as opposed to simply interchangeable humanoids is to try and grasp at a knowledge of myself as much as it is to understand why those friends like me in return. I struggled with this essay for months. It wasn't until I was channel surfing one night and happened to linger upon a PBS show about string theory that I found a framework to talk about what friendship means to me.

Very successfully, this program rendered the concept of string theory in such a way that a totally math-impaired individual like me could understand it. I was never a student who hoped to aspire to an

On the Meaning of Friendship Between Gay Men

understanding of the world from the aspect of something as complicated as physics. My way of perceiving the world is much more
ephemeral and transitory. Yet, the show helped me to understand that
the universe exists simultaneously as the very large and the very
small. We understand that world based on three dimensions plus time.
We have up and down, left and right, in and out, plus time. It's like
this: I can place myself in the real world using these simple things.
For instance, I have a doctor's appointment at 9:45 a.m. on Thursday.
I can navigate through the seen world by traveling along a series of
lefts and rights to my doctor's office. I can go into his building and up
one flight of stairs in order to arrive at precisely 9:45 a.m. This is a
three-dimensional experience within the reference of time.

So far, so good. String theory allows for the other descriptions of
my experience at the doctor's office because string theory allows for
other dimensions and, in my way of thinking, these other dimensions
encompass the variety of human interaction. You see, string theory
holds that at the subatomic, subquark level, all matter is composed of
separate, distinct strands of energy that are vibrating along at their individual frequency. It is the harmonious symphony of all these minute
vibrations that make up the world as we see it. Now think about it: As
different as we all are from one another, each vibrating along at our
individual frequency of reality, we encounter others at different
points in time whose vibrations complement our own. For a space in
time we synch harmoniously to create common affinities. Thus, out
of the whole human race, we encounter others with whom we synch
up and create a shared reality.

Big idea, huh? In a way, it seems an unwieldy way to describe how
I come to meet someone at Starbucks for a half-hour's conversation,
but at the same time, it's a rather elegant argument for how I'd chose
to interact with that person at all. You see, I'm one of those people
who has very little affinity for others. I am a loner. For a variety of
reasons, I have never found it easy to make friends much less sustain
friendships over long periods of time. I have always been perfectly
happy vibrating away at my own frequency as a separate, discrete en-
tity. I rather like the idea that my particular reality is unique. I enjoy
thinking that I am alone in my expression of being. That I find others
with whom I vibrate synchronistically is a pretty cool thought as well,
given how little effort I actually make to meet and find those people.

I wish I could say that simply being gay has influenced my ideas of my individual uniqueness, but that's too easy. Many gay people experience a sense of isolation and alienation by way of being ostracized and excluded from others beginning as far back as childhood, but there is a huge gay community out there with everything from Web sites to potluck suppers to encourage a shared common identity and to provide opportunities for human interaction and intimacy.

One factor that has a more complex effect on my interactions with others is chronic mental illness. I am essentially a high-functioning crazy person. I am not comfortable inviting others to share my life as friends because I live in a world that is bound by more dimensions than are commonly accepted as normal. Human interaction for me has always had the same impediments as trying to speak to someone in a nonnative language. If I am forced to speak French, all of my conversation has to go through a mental translation before I speak, groping at both allusion and vocabulary to make myself understood. I don't beg any sympathy for this. It's just my way of relating to people and, more often than not, I don't find it worth the effort.

The amazing thing to me is that I have friends at all. Yet, there are others who value my company, my insights, and who appreciate the way I see the world. These people, these friends, are vibrating harmoniously in their own isolation with my energy. For some good reason, we connect. Let me give you an example.

A few weeks ago, I got a call from a friend of mine I'll call Rhonda. We became friends through my partner, who has known Rhonda for many years. As a consequence, I've known Rhonda for nearly fifteen years myself. On the surface, there is very little reason for us to be friends. Rhonda is sixty-seven years old. She has four children and four grandchildren. She's been married her whole life to the same man she fell in love with in junior high school. Rhonda lives three towns away and has a very busy life. We only see each other perhaps a half dozen times a year.

One Monday night, she called me and left a message on my voicemail saying she wanted to talk to me before she chickened out and could I call her back as soon as possible. I returned the call the following morning. We chatted awhile before she told me she really wanted to get together with me for a visit. She sounded anxious, so I asked her if she wanted to come over that afternoon. She accepted my invitation gratefully and so I cleared my schedule for her.

Rhonda came over about one o'clock and sat at my kitchen table for the next three hours and poured her heart out over the course of a pot of coffee and many cigarettes. In her world, so separate and discrete from mine, there was much that was troubling about which I had no idea. All I really did was sit and listen, offering her some encouragement and complete and total acceptance and understanding. Rhonda told me that I was the only person she could imagine talking to about what was so wrong in her world, and she knew I would neither judge her nor repeat any of what we had discussed. She left saying she felt much better and that I had saved her life.

I was glad that I had the time and opportunity to visit with Rhonda. She's a great person and I would like to see her free of the problems that have her tormented right now. I hope I was some help, as a listener and comforter if nothing else.

What amazes me, and what I think my appropriation of string theory to explain the meaning of friendship is all about, is how Rhonda came to choose me, from the entire constellation of her relationships, to confide in and to seek comfort from. In the randomness of the world and the way we achieve intimacy with others, there has to be some explanation for the Rhondas in my world. There comes a time when the vibration of my frequency attracts that of others and in that attraction the effect is beneficial and harmonious for both me and Rhonda. Meaningful people in my life occur for this very reason. I have no other explanation for it.

As for me, I rarely reach out to others for comfort, approbation, or encouragement. The life experiences that formed me, informed me that I would be best served by finding those things from within. Growing up both gay and chronically mentally ill, I found few I could trust with the harsh and private beauty my own perceptions provided. It is strange that I make my living with words. The fictions and works of my imagination are often very real to me. But then, I have been a translator all my life. To write a book is nothing more than the disciplined practice of translating what I see in my head and offering it as a means of expressing myself to the larger world we commonly agree to call real. The product of the effort is at a comfortable remove from my reality and who I am most privately. I am lucky to have the outlet.

Likewise, I am lucky to have my friend Joe. I actually wrote a book about our friendship six years ago titled *The Mentor: A Memoir of Friendship and Gay Identity*. It was my first successful published work. We've been friends now for twenty-five years and he's one of few people with whom I have a common, ongoing compatibility sustained over many long years and many miles between us. These days, Joe lives in Petersburg, Virginia and commutes into Richmond each day to work. At least three times a week, he calls me to keep him company on his drive home. It is a part of my day I look forward to.

Joe and I have shared many of the experiences of our adult lives. We hold each other's history in a way that transcends friendship and approaches the familial. When I die, I can honestly say Joe was one of the handful of people who actually knew me. When I try to wrap my mind around the meaning of that friendship, I feel as if I'm trying to contemplate the simultaneous simplicity and complexity of string theory. It simply is. It confounds me that I managed to make and maintain such a friendship over so long a time. My friend Joe is at all the boundaries of my known world. Grief and elation, love and loss, triumph and struggle, Joe has shared it all with me, graciously and with great kindness that sometimes has been undeserved.

Our friendships are better described as affinities that are strong or weak, but measurable within the ever-expanding ripples on the pond of our consciousness. I like the idea of vibrating along at a frequency that joins with others to create harmonies in the dissonance of my existence. Ultimately, that's what our friends are. They represent a completion of our individual singularity. They come not to dilute our selves, but to complement them. When, like string theory supposes, you track and trace down the essential energies of which we are made, the path to that place is lit by the gleam of other's energies. Just as I can't possibly be as totally self-absorbed as I imagine myself to be if there is a Rhonda for me to comfort and console, or a Joe for me to share a joke only we can get, I exist in some ways only through my ability to respond to the energies that dance discretely all around me.

That's my thinking on the meaning of friendship. For me, string theory is as good an explanation as any.

13

Not Quite There

Felice Picano

During the 1960s and 1970s, it became commonplace, even cliché, to say of someone you didn't quite understand that he or she was "far out" or "from outer space." I certainly met more than my share of these folks, and indeed to some people, at times I myself was considered "out there" and "far out." In fact, once our little urban commune was going on West 13th Street, our housemother—and drug dispenser—Margaret D., took to calling me "Philly, you're so far out!" smushed all together like that, so that newcomers thought it was my name, and repeated the entire phrase addressing me until I managed to correct them. But I knew from far out myself, and among the very many far out people I met during this period, few compared to Bobby Brown. But rather than refer to Bobby as a space cadet or moonwalker as so many others did, I thought of him in terms, not so much of great distance, but instead of deficit, lack, or scarcity, in short, as "not quite there." It was an inadequacy I recognized easily enough, while never precisely comprehending what it entailed. And despite probing, I never quite figured out how it had come about.

I first met Bobby when he was living over a health food store on 11th Street off 6th Avenue in the heart of the Village. My pal George Sampson brought me there to meet his brother and sister, Bernie and Anne Sampson, and we entered while they were all in the middle of a card game called "Hell." This consisted of four- or five-handed Solitaire, played with as many decks as players, with all the cards to be taken off a single giant pile, the participants seated around it on the floor. The object of the game was to complete your lines first. Naturally, everyone grabbing for cards aroused hostilities, since two, sometimes three players, might want a particular card and grab for it;

On the Meaning of Friendship Between Gay Men

and especially on drugs—methedrine was the drug of choice here—
the players could get loud, abusive, even violent. That was, of course,
the "fun" of it.

Away from the game, being host, Bobby Brown was a smidgen
calmer, though a wire-strung edge ran evident in him from the very
first. We'd only just met at his apartment door, when he turned and
screeched, "Bernie! Stop cheating!"

I could tell he'd prefer being in the game and we let him go back
to it.

A few weeks before Christmas 1970, following two years in which
I'd not seen him, Bobby telephoned and said that someone wanted to
turn the health food store below his apartment into a two-story health
food restaurant. They were buying him out of his lease. But he had to
move out quickly: by the end of December. He'd been looking for an
apartment in the area and had located a long-leased place. But it
wouldn't be vacant until April first and he'd been unable to find a sub-
let. He knew that George and I were good friends. He also understood—from whom, he'd never specified and George was gone from
Manhattan by then—that I was out of work and could use someone to
share the rent with.

I was and I could. Yet I still hemmed and hawed. I didn't really
want a roommate, much as I knew it would financially help me out. I
valued—perhaps overvalued—my privacy.

Mistaking my reluctance as hesitation because we didn't know
each other, Bobby suggested we meet, I suppose so he could try to
dispel any doubts I might have about him. We did meet, in my apartment; we smoked a joint together and drank beer and, looking around
the place, Bobby told me he thought he and I had pretty similar life-
styles. He was very easygoing, he said. Sitting there, with his relaxed,
lanky, almost muscleless, pale-skinned, East Texas body, his dirty
blonde hair worn "Dutch boy," and his mellow "country" voice, he
actually seemed to be the person he presented to me.

That much established, Bobby more closely looked over my apartment, discussing how he might transform my former-dining-room
now-study into his room. He worked somewhere, he told me, although he wasn't crystal clear about it, so I wasn't sure if it was a head
shop, a poster shop, or what—from six in the evening until midnight.
That meant I'd be alone, free to write without anyone being in the
apartment during those hours. I had to admit that was a real plus in

Bobby's favor. He thought he might hook a curtain across the open doorway between the study and living room, he said, so I could use the living room to work in, even when he was home.

He was so much calmer and more sedate than when I'd last seen him that I was strongly tempted. The fact that he actually alluded to those card games, made my decision easier. "I don't use speed or play 'Hell' anymore," he assured me, as gravely as his grandpappy might have assured his bride-to-be that he'd stopped cattle rustling and distilling his own "corn-likker."

Even so, again I said I'd think about it. But Bobby phoned two days later and *had* to have an answer. Pressured, broke, I said, sure, he could move in: for three months.

Thus ensued the oddest of my roommates. He arrived with two cats he'd completely forgotten to mention: "Speed" and "Skag," who were twin brothers, Bobby said, *and* homosexual. It only took a single afternoon to appreciate their names. One was hyper and nervous; the other was so idle he might as well be a statue. They ignored each other weeks at a go. Until, that is, they fought. Then they chased each other around the apartment hours at a time, stopping only to hiss, screech, and claw madly. These fights invariably ended with them nuzzling and making up. I would usually remain vibrating for another hour.

Bobby also brought with him cardboard box after cardboard box of undefined stuff which he used—brick-like—to construct a thick, if somewhat unstable, wall between the living room and study, with just enough space for him to pass through, all of it covered by a double curtain. Bobby hung dark swaths of fabric over everything in his room, which, along with the usually dim lighting, meant I could never quite make out what he actually had in there. An opaque shade was fixed onto the window so tightly no light would dream of entering. Another friend, in later years, called his dark bedroom "The Tomb of Ligea," after the Poe story. But Bobby Brown's was the original.

Along with all this darkness and containment, Bobby also brought a reel-to-reel tape player, tape reels, books, notebooks, marijuana, and who knows what other stimulants. Of all the druggies I knew at that time—and there were a legion—he turned out to be by far the most methodical: he even had the latest pharmacists' "Blue Book" of current prescription pills.

Bobby might have stopped using speed, but he was definitely on something most of the time. He would awaken at two p.m. If I were in the adjoining living room (now dining room and study, too) and I didn't have my stereo earphones on, I would hear him stirring behind the curtain, and some time afterward—often a half hour later—he would draw open the curtain. Sometimes he would reheat coffee I'd made earlier or brew his own pot. He never drank enough of it to account for how strangely wired he quickly became.

Despite my repeated invitations to come out into the bright, sunny living room, Bobby would remain pretty much in that dim little room until it was getting dark out and it was time for him to fix something to eat and go to work. On weekends, he seldom strayed from his room until quite late at night. With his pale appearance, almost colorless blond hair, and thin, nearly boneless body, he might easily have been a contemporary vampire.

Except that Bobby Brown was, in his own weird, completely individual way, touching, funny, and totally endearing. Demons definitely lurked within, even if they seemed to be directed mainly at Bobby himself. His cackling laugh was harshest when he was laughing at some newly revealed flaw in himself or at something he'd said or done. His quiet, intense, completely spelled-out hatreds, which escalated fiercely in conversation before utterly dying away as he lighted another Winston or pipeful of hashish, would eventually return to lodge—and grate—in his own breast. His general demeanor could be best described as world-weary, which I have to admit in those days I found substantially more compatible than if he'd been perky.

But while I and my friends were half playacting at being cynical and *deracinee*, Bobby wasn't playing at anything. Although he was only a few years older than me and had been out in the world either as long or less than I'd been, he was already utterly fatigued by it all. Then, there were those times, that I'd be speaking on the phone or cooking and I would suddenly catch him looking at me the way an aged grandparent with a fatal, wasting disease gazes at a perfectly healthy grandchild. He possessed a sort of wearied indulgence: he might admire my cheerful naïveté, but he would not think to emulate it.

Bobby moving in with me helped solve the worst of my financial problems and he didn't much intrude on my life. He did provide a bit of companionship—despite the few hours he was awake, or at home with the curtain open. So it was weeks before other, less healthy, aspects of his personality emerged. Maybe there were hints of it all the time but I was then so preoccupied with trying to make work a three-way relationship with two other men that I probably was oblivious to those early signs.

One afternoon, a month after he'd moved in, Bobby said to me in what I had already come to recognize as his most querulous tone of voice, "I never get mail! Since the day I moved in here, I haven't gotten any mail. I put in a change of address. And yet, no mail!"

It was such an obvious accusation and so patently absurd, that I decided to defuse it totally. I replied casually, "You get mail. I burn it."

I thought his eyes would pop out of his head. His voice became a hoarse whisper. At long last, he uttered, "Why would you burn my mail?"

"Excellent question. Why *would* I burn your mail?" I asked back, Socratically I hoped.

He thought a longish time, then said in a more normal tone of voice. "I'll go to the Post Office and put through another change of address."

"That's a good idea," I replied, casually. End of conversation.

A few days later his mail poured in.

But if that bit of unadulterated paranoia was one hint of Bobby's growing cocaine use, it was by no means the last. Whatever Bobby Brown's own personal demons might be, they had the result of bringing out unsavory effects in the atmosphere immediately adjoining him. For one, my Jane Street apartment poltergeist, which had resided there long before he arrived but had mercifully lain dormant. Once Bobby was in residence, the poltergeist began to act up a great deal—usually with him as victim.

Forget the special-effects movies you've seen: this was the real thing. As a rule both subtle and unobtrusive, it would suddenly come to life, depending upon the person in residence. A few days after I'd first moved in, I was in the bedroom reading *The Guermantes Way,* when I became aware of a constant, even insistent, sound in the living room. It wasn't loud, but it was *invariable* and therefore became really irritating. When I jumped up and went to see what the sound was, it turned out to have a source that was invisible and inexplicable.

I searched the backyard. I listened at each wall for mice. I did everything I could and that anyone else would do to locate the sound. With no success. And, of course, once I was up, the sound stopped. Five minutes later, I was in the bedroom reading again and the noise was back. Subtle at first, then definitely there. It sounded like, well, the closest I could arrive at how it sounded was like sand falling in a tightly closed space. I tapped the walls to see if maybe plaster was dropping. No. Nothing there. But it was awfully irritating! I checked other possibilities. Nothing. Yet every time I went back to my bedroom to read, it started up again.

It happened a fourth time. Annoyed beyond belief, I leapt up, ran into the living room and shouted at nothing, at no one, nowhere, "Shut up! This is *my* apartment. *I* pay the rent! Shut up! You can make all the noise you want when I'm *out*. When I'm here, you will *shut up!* Do you hear?"

When I returned to my bedroom to delve again into Proust's complex syntax, the noise did not repeat. And I guess it was that instant apparent obedience that confirmed somewhere in my mind the idea that some-thing was actually in the apartment, although it would be years before I even found a name to give it. I also thought about who had lived there before me—poor, stressed-out, hapless Joan Estoup; and I recalled the so-called curse put on her by a witch. Subsequent to this incident, and my screaming, the sound never recurred and so I naturally forgot all about it.

Until that is, Bobby Brown moved in. Suddenly the apartment's revenant was reactivated. First, Bobby began complaining about strange dreams, nightmares in which he was inside the apartment, running for his life, running from something shadowy, menacing.

A day or two days after he told me of the dream, the two of us were on my bed together, lying on our stomachs, looking through *Rolling Stone* magazine and we heard footsteps along the short corridor from the apartment door to the living room. My bedroom door was mostly shut and I at first thought I'd left the door to the apartment open and someone had walked in. I got up to check. There was no one there. Hmm, I thought, *that's* odd.

Thereafter I'd often hear those footsteps while I was in my bedroom reading or laying awake in bed, hear them step along eight feet of hallway, always going in the same direction. I'd jump up to look. There was never anyone there.

One day I came home to find an opaque new shower curtain had been put up. My transparent one really had needed replacing, it was so streaked and foggy, so I thanked Bobby for this bright new one.

He looked balefully at me and said, "It makes no difference. I took a shower before and I still feel like someone's watching me."

As soon as he said it, I realized that I also felt like someone was watching me whenever I was in the shower; even with the bathroom door closed; even when I knew I was alone in the apartment. In fact since Bobby had moved in, more than once from the bathtub, I would hear a few footsteps along the hallway, then feel right through the closed bathroom door someone looking at me. It was subtle, eerie. In later years, all sorts of friends would volunteer having experienced the same eldritch sensation. One guest of a friend who subletted my place for an entire summer month became so terrified that neither of them ended up sleeping there.

"What do you think it could be?" I asked Bobby one afternoon.

He was sitting up in bed, smoking a joint.

He turned with a deadly look and said, "My cats run from it."

"Didn't you go look to see if anything was there?" I asked.

"Hell no!" His eyes huge with horror. "I just hoped it wouldn't come closer." He went on to tell me that it acted up the most when I wasn't home. But, he added, while the footsteps came to within inches of the separating curtain, they never came into the study, explaining why he always kept to that room.

"Yell at it," I said. "That's what I did before."

Bobby said he was afraid his yelling would sound more fearful than furious. "It knows," he whispered as though someone were hearing what we said.

I was more amused than anything. But the poltergeist's intrusion slowly escalated and I found that at last, I had to intervene.

One afternoon there was a phone call for Bobby, and the long telephone wires in the living room had become so twisted through use that they no longer stretched to reach his bed. He stood and talked on the phone, as I attempted to untangle the wires.

The call was an upsetting one for him: either he had to go to work early, or stay later, or work an extra shift. After he hung up, he dropped into my bentwood rocking chair, fulminating, while I continued to kneel to try to untwist the phone wire. A second later, Bobby leapt out of the chair and almost knocked me over trying to get into the study.

"Did you see that? Did you?" he demanded. "It jerked back the chair! I almost fell out. It's after me!" he wailed. He couldn't be talked out of it.

I lied and said I was going to find a magic spell to get rid of it. A few days later I said I'd done it, exorcised the poltergeist. Bobby clearly didn't believe me and while he didn't complain of it any more, both of us now secretly began counting the days until April first, when he'd be moving out.

Winter suddenly turned nasty, snowy, wet. The little bit of company Bobby Brown had provided dwindled to nothing. After work ended at midnight, he would go out with friends, not get home until six in the morning, then not wake up until shortly before he had to go to work at five p.m. Most of our contact was limited to his increasingly cocaine-assisted *levees*. And on nicer days, I'd already be out of doors by the time those occurred and so I came to more and more miss even those peculiar nonevents.

Bobby moved out of my apartment and into his own place two weeks early, taking with him half the rent. I didn't realize until he was gone what a small, persistent drain he had been on my attention and on my sense of well-being. Once he'd gotten all his boxes out of my study, I tore down the sheets of dark cloth he'd swathed the room in and pulled off the tape with which he'd closed out light from the window. I swept and vacuumed the little room, flung open a window to air it out, and light rushed back into the apartment and back into my life.

And there it might have all ended. Except that Bobby didn't completely vanish. Through infrequent letters and phone calls with George Sampson—our original connection—I discovered that Bobby had not stayed in his new Village apartment for the full length of the lease—his purported intention—but instead moved uptown to a railroad flat in a tenement building in the East Eighties. Through someone else—Miss Sherry maybe—I then heard that Bobby was living with a woman. And from Douglas Brashears or was it Chuck Partridge, I heard the surprising news that Bobby had married her. As I'd never before suspected that Bobby was anything but gay—if indeed he possessed any brand of sexuality, which seemed pretty dubious— this information baffled me as much as it bored me. A few more years passed.

By the mid-1970s, my life had become relatively different than it had been when I'd first met Bobby. I was now a successfully published author, and I'd moved out of the little back apartment on Jane Street into a much airier and handsomer Federal Era duplex several blocks further west. I seldom saw many of the people I'd known earlier—mostly their doing as I continued to try to stay in touch. I did spend half of each year—usually all summer—living in Fire Island Pines. Then I began spending winters outside New York City, too—in San Francisco, Key West, or Los Angeles. As a result, my socializing completely altered. After a few years I seldom saw or heard from any of my Sixties friends, except infrequently, or by accident, encountered on street corners or outside theater lobbies. So I was very surprised one summery late March morning in 1979 to get a phone call from Bobby. He was nearby he said, only a few blocks away, and he wanted to talk to me.

His voice sounded a little slurred, but I couldn't think what from at this early hour. (It was 10:30 a.m.) He said he had a nearby appointment—doctor? job interview? I wondered—but would come by in an hour and he would pick up a six-pack of beer, he said; was that okay? Feeling curious and a little guilty about having allowed Bobby to disappear so totally from my life, I said, sure, okay, come on by.

Bobby looked the same as a decade earlier. Almost precisely the same. I was aware that I looked quite different than when he'd last seen me. Then, I'd been broke for years on end, and as a result, thin, with a full beard, and longish hair. Now I was well-fed, even muscular, tanned from a winter in Southern California, with short hair, expensive casual clothing, and a mustache. He still resembled a drugged-out hippie, whereas I looked like a Fire Island Clone with disposable income—which was pretty much what I was.

I wondered why, on this very warm day, Bobby was wearing a long-sleeve shirt. He looked around my vast new apartment with a certain wry amusement: the fireplaces, the fourteen-foot ceilings, the custom-made bookshelves, the foot-high crown moldings, the Turkish carpets, and handmade coffee table. Virtually all the older furniture he'd known was gone, replaced several years ago. Only a bentwood rocking chair and a dark wood gateleg table that served for writing and eating and card games when placed in front of a twelve-foot-long polished oak church pew I'd found on the street remained from the old place—both pieces downstairs in the new apartment. It was the same bentwood rocker Bobby used to sit in, the same one he claimed to have been jerked out of by a poltergeist. It now sat unused in a dim corner of my huge new downstairs dining room, while the gate-leg served as a butler's table between the new kitchen and dining room.

When Bobby saw the two old pieces, he decided we should stay downstairs, even though it was dark and closed in, especially compared to the brilliantly sunny living room upstairs, with its high windows dominated by the white powder puffs of three flowering pear trees outside.

I opened the downstairs windows an inch while he was in the bathroom, then I pulled up a chair opposite where he'd established his space: the rocker at the table. A nice breeze began to blow, but as he exited the bathroom, he ignored it. He put the six-pack in the fridge, minus one for each of us. During the ensuing hour-long visit, Bobby drank four more beers.

At first, I imagined that it was a purely social visit. Bobby did ask a few questions about me and about my life. He had heard a little bit, from someone or other, about my success: when he'd known me I was just beginning to write. In the decade since, I'd published three novels, with a fourth about to come out that fall. The previous summer, my second book, *Eyes*, was a paperback bestseller: I couldn't go anywhere in the city without seeing someone reading it. Bobby must have seen it, too. He didn't mention that, and not being too egotistical, I quickly moved the topic of conversation from me, to him and his life, saying that I'd heard he'd gotten married.

"That's over," Bobby said. "It's all over. In fact, the reason I came by is . . ." he rocked in the bentwood and looked at me and sipped his beer, "You know, I'm seeing a therapist. Right here in your neighborhood. Ever since, well, she thinks I should inspect my past and see what the possibilities were then so I can see what they might be."

That explained the appointment that brought him downtown. But despite a handful of questions, I still found what he was saying incomprehensible. Bobby finished one beer, got another, and began on that. When, in the midst of talking, he finally noticed my puzzlement, he put down the beer and rolled up his sleeves. On his wrists were thick bandages.

"Look!" he said in his most familiarly querulous tone of voice. "I tried to commit suicide a couple weeks ago. We had yet another fight and I couldn't stand my life anymore, and I went up to the roof of the apartment building with a big knife, and I slashed my wrists. And you know what? When the blood began to just gush out, to just jet out, I got so scared, I began shouting. And even though I passed out, they found me and took me to the hospital."

I had known three people who'd committed suicide in recent years. I told him so. I also said maybe it was a good thing that he'd stopped himself.

Bobby finished his beer, got another one, popped it open, and drank it down. "No," he said with that country-Texas definiteness I remembered. "I don't think so. I was just chicken-shit. I'm off drugs now. Completely. Totally. And I really *hate* being off drugs. They were the only thing that made being alive worthwhile. I hate being straight and married. But I also hate being queer. I hate working. And I hate doing nothing all day. I just really hate being alive. You understand what I mean, don't you?"

I didn't know how to respond and said so. I told Bobby that I was finally living the kind of life I had wanted for years. I didn't hate being alive. And I loved being queer. Although I could understand someone else maybe not loving it. But wait, wasn't there anything Bobby wanted? Wasn't there anything to strive for? To have as a goal?

He lifted one of the bandages to show me the wide, thick, barely healed scars across his veins. He opened another beer and drank it down. He told me he would probably try to kill himself again. And he was coming to see me to tell me, well, he didn't know *what* it was that he wanted to tell me. He had no idea why he'd called me and why he'd come by today. Except he'd been in the neighborhood, at that therapist's office, and he'd remembered the phone number and he thought it might be a good idea.

He drank the fourth beer, rocking back and forth, the two of us silent, then he got up and left. He hugged me awkwardly at the door. And Bobby smelled, I don't know, somehow like a little boy smells. Someone seven or eight years old. Not like a grown man of nearly forty.

I remember thinking about him for the next few days. But whenever I did, it was with that resigned consciousness one has about something that is already consummated. I'd always known something inside Bobby was chasing after him, and I'd come to believe that somehow, because of my apartment, and possibly even because of me being there, whatever was chasing Bobby had coalesced into a recognizable force those few months we'd lived together. What it was, exactly, and how to get rid of it, I didn't understand, although clearly by now Bobby had alienated himself totally. From me. From his closest friends, George and Anne Sampson. Even from his wife.

I'd known other young men who had killed themselves. But they'd had reasons. One was a handsome young marine, who found out he was gay, went AWOL after the Christmas holidays, and hung himself from a sixth-story plant hook jutting out from a concrete balcony of the upscale Van Gogh apartment building where he'd been staying with a gay couple who'd befriended him. I'd come home from dancing all night and stepped out of the cab onto the utterly desolated corner of Jane and Hudson Streets at 5:10 in the morning and I'd instantly seen him hanging there, his body sort of flapping against the side of the building. I'd known who it was and why he'd done it. The cabbie called the cops. But I was exhausted and didn't wait around until they arrived.

Another handsome, slender young man I knew, who used to date my barber, also killed himself—in fact, spent most of a particular afternoon killing himself—slashing his wrists and neck, trying to hang himself, and finally throwing himself off the roof of the 23rd Street YMCA. I'd spent little time with him, but I vividly recalled this reserved, shy, quiet guy suddenly opening up to me one evening as we rode home together side by side on the privately owned Fire Island to Manhattan bus. Even though he had seemingly everything to live for and to look forward to, he told me that he felt like a total stranger, a fake human, an alien. After explaining how enviably ordinary and filled with good things his life had been, he concluded, "But I'm not like other people." He said it with quiet, insistent passion. And when I tried to explain how similar that was to many young people, he answered, "No! You don't understand. This body feels all wrong to me. And the sky—and the water—everything here's the wrong color, the wrong consistency, the wrong odor! I think I was born into the wrong species. Or born on the wrong planet. That's possible, right?"

Nothing so life-defining or life-threatening for Bobby Brown. When he first moved in, I was so perplexed by his nihilistic attitude toward life that I eagerly searched for clues within the scanty information about himself Bobby had told me of his past life and growing up. He'd come from East Texas. His mother separated from his father, who had then moved, following oil drilling west, and never came back. Bobby's mother and he had been close, especially as he was an only child, but she was sickly and they'd moved to her parent's homestead, where she died of tuberculosis. Yet he didn't speak about her death as the tragedy that had ruined his life. He didn't particulary miss his father or older male company either. Bobby had been raised by his grandmother. He had no stories about her or how she'd raised him to suggest that she was particularly kind and loving or peculiarly cruel and monstrous toward him. He had no stories about his childhood at all. I'd tell him about my childhood, and he'd rock in the bentwood and smoke his hash pipe and not have anything to offer by way of reply. Since Bobby was given to instant, thorough, and at times extremely fault-finding analyses of his friends, I would expect him to say something about anyone who had even dreamed of mistreating him while growing up. So I explored his past in our conversation. And I came up with no one and nothing to account for his dark moods. He'd done okay in high school. Had no tales of it to tell. Had no first-time sex stories to relate as a kid. Perhaps his best times had been his first two years in college. He spoke of those days with a restrained sense of pleasure. But all I could figure out as a potential cause was when Bobby first had sex with other guys and got turned on to pot. He'd left college after two years, offering no reason why.

The summer of 1980, following Bobby's inexplicable beer-drinking visit, while I was home overnight from Fire Island transacting business, I received a phone call from his ex-wife. Bobby Brown had finally accomplished something he'd really wanted in life: he'd at last succeeded in killing himself. She said that Bobby had taken sleeping pills and put a plastic garment bag over his head. She sounded distraught, yet hardened too, so I assumed that I must be about the tenth or twelfth person she had called with the news.

His ex-wife promised to call again and let me know when Bobby was being memorialized or buried and where the funeral or memorial would be held. I was visiting friends in Los Angeles for the next few weeks and, if she ever phoned, I must have missed the call.

14

The Absence:
Living Everyday Life
Without Gay Male Friends

Eric Aoki

A longing for cultural identification and moments of interpersonal loneliness are two things that come to mind when I think about the everyday absence of gay male friendships. At this moment, I cannot name one gay male friend present in my life in Fort Collins, Colorado, the city where I work and live roughly nine months of the year. In fact, my friends often watch me struggle living amidst a predominantly straight community, a comfortable and good life, albeit one mostly absent of out gay men like myself. Although I have several gay male acquaintances through my ties to the university and local volunteer organizations, none are individuals with whom I have established close or long-term friendships. The three I know are either much like me—busy and constantly on the go—or less like me— settled into long-term coupled lives, or quite simply, much more private individuals than I. In the end, however, I simply do not know these men or their lives well enough to call them friends.[1]

In this essay, I reflect on the absence of gay male friendships, illuminating my experiences in the cultural spaces I inhabit and participate in as an often perceived cultural other. I explore three related questions: (1) What are the implications for choosing to live in a locale where the demographic of out gay men is relatively invisible or absent? (2) What concerns and adjustments come with being the sole openly out gay man in my own circle of long-term, local friends?

On the Meaning of Friendship Between Gay Men

(3) What sociocultural imperatives call for enhanced connections in and through gay male friendships?

Cultural Locale and the Absence of Gay Male Presence and Visibility

> During the latter half of the seventeenth century—that pivotal period for the emergence of modern society—several hundred coffee houses opened up in London alone. . . . A small number of these coffee houses were called molly houses and they served a particular clientele: a male homosexual subculture with a rather different agenda. . . . It is perhaps only going slightly too far to say that the men who frequented them carried the remembrance of a way of relating between men that might otherwise have been increasingly excluded during this time of social change. If we ask tongue in cheek, what was the significance of these homosexuals to society at large, the answer in a word is friendship.
>
> Vernon, 2005, p. 130

Logically, I understand that where I have chosen to live and play out my academic career places me in an area that is demographically challenged or absent of a cultural scene with any significant presence of other out gay men. I have told myself that I make this life choice because, in the mindset of a rural, working-class kid who had the goal of climbing the academic ladder, I was hired into an ideal position that offered upward mobility within an outstanding department that houses nationally and internationally recognized colleagues. Additionally, when I accepted this position in 1997, I believed that the diversity of my identity and perspective—a gay, U.S. ethnic minority, working class to professional class, and a Catholic and Buddhist— were important to share somewhere, academically, so that my cultural identity and experiences might help build bridges of understanding through stimulating classroom dialogue. (I teach co-cultural, intercultural, and interpersonal communication classes.) After nine years, I still believe that my presence and interactions with students and many members of the Fort Collins community continue to serve this purpose. In essence, however, I accepted a position at a predominantly White, American university that matriculates students who avow, generally, to the same cultural composition as the dominant diversity variables visible in the larger Fort Collins community (i.e., middle to upper-middle class social status and heterosexual/heteronormative orientation and practices).

During this time, I have remained committed to a department and to the many memorable students who have, in turn, helped me to better understand the intersection of my professional, gay, and multicultural identities. My academic department, colleagues, and Old Town Fort Collins community have been supportive to me as a university professor, a friend, a neighbor, and an individual of multiple visible and avowed cultural diversities—variables that easily mark me as the "other."

Having noted these differences, my day-to-day life is one that I consider privileged, since I am known within the Old Town community as a friendly neighbor and an engaged, successful academic. I am also often acknowledged for being civic-minded, diversity-engaged, arts-supportive, and global-influenced. I am known as someone who enjoys local cultural events and interacting with many people. So, when I focus on the quality of people and experiences that my life and networks afford, I feel very fortunate.

With so much going well, I have always been puzzled with my feeling of emptiness or lack of cultural identification, holistically, within the city at large. Hence, I have worked hard to construct a safe space in my art studio, Studio 23, in the heart of Old Town Fort Collins, a place where friends, university colleagues, and community allies come to mix and mingle amidst art, queer presence, diverse groups, and conversation. Nevertheless, I often feel a void living here.

When asked if I miss my family or miss interacting with individuals of my ethnicity and social-class background, I often say yes without hesitation. When asked if I feel a loss living in a predominantly heterosexual and heteronormative community, I often feel the pressure to say no in order to avoid sounding overly discontent with my choice to be where I am. But, in truth, the answer is also yes, even with all of my wonderful and supportive straight friends and allies. In fact, at this juncture, living without gay male friends is the more challenging loss of identification to work through whenever I return from my frequent travel escapes. Finding ethnic minority connection happens a bit more easily and publicly.

Despite all of this, I believe it is counterproductive to label my friendships in Fort Collins as consisting almost exclusively of straight people, but I believe the labeling does speak to an accurate, perhaps strongly pronounced, makeup of friends in my daily life. And, I believe I would not notice the absence of gay male friends within my circles and networks if in fact I had any.

Mostly I miss being in cultural spaces where gay people are more visible. Even during a recent summer family trip to Mexico City, within an hour of wandering through the gay-friendly Zona Rosa, we passed at least five gay male couples walking hand in hand, and one polite, gay man chatted me up as I waited for my family to finish shopping.

At that moment, I thought, wow, already an opportunity to be-friend another gay male! As is typically the case during these last nine years, I travel the globe, most often to larger cities, to more easily find and engage gay men for conversation about our lives and potential friendship.

As one of my women friends[2] in Fort Collins often notes, the men I befriend or who befriend me either avow as straight—albeit straight men who are supportive allies—or are men with whom I have had sexual relations.[3] My friend, nonetheless, is quick to point out how absent gay male friendships are in my life. She has even posed a queer version of the *When Harry Met Sally* friends-and-lovers dilemma with me. Although I believe she is onto something regarding gay men, sexual relations, and the ability to negotiate friendship with each other, I believe the equation leaves out the paucity of gay men, demographically, to even begin addressing these issues. So, in es-sence, I tell her that given where we live, we must first start with a more basic twist to the relational question: "Will Eric Ever Even Get to Meet More Gay Men to See if They Can Coexist as Friends?"

Somewhere along the way I learned that to admit to feeling at a loss without a queer community somehow demonstrates a lack of per-sonal strength. I believe this perspective stems from the hetero-normative-instilled mindset of: "I don't need gay people to feel good about myself or to live life." Many of my straight acquaintances and friends understand, perhaps even empathize, with missing my family of origin and cultural connections to my ethnic-social roots in Cali-fornia or the more cosmopolitan, diverse cities that I often visit. But it seems more challenging to get people to understand how much I can also miss being around a family of people who share my sexual orientation, that is, gay male friendships often formed as a chosen family when coming out. Nardi (1999) asserts the importance of these connections of identification:

> Friendship networks are the avenues through which gay social worlds are constructed, the sites upon which gay men's identities and communities are formed and where the quotidian dimensions of our lives are carried out . . . Friendship may be the central organizing element of gay men's lives—the mechanism through which gay masculinities, gay identities, gay cultures, and gay neighborhoods get created, transformed, maintained, and reproduced. (p. 13)

Presently, I have no gay men in my daily life with whom I identify or look to for support. Those with whom I am friends are either distant geographically or generationally. This is by no means a negative. I simply do not have many gay male friends who understand my day-to-day life or who identify with my generation. I do have a couple of older gay men friends, who have mentored me and taught me the history and struggles of our identities as well as numerous younger university students who have come out in my classes and who have maintained a connection after graduating and moving on to other cultural contexts, generally San Francisco and San Diego. But the potential to build friendships day-to-day with other gay men is obviously limited.

Through contemporary popular culture I also learned, and even expected, that my life might be more like the gay male friendship circles (re)presented in popular shows and films such as *Love! Valor! Compassion!*, *The Broken Hearts Club*, *Queer as Folk*, and even *Angels in America*. Yet, I have rarely-to-never experienced these types of families. These days, I often wonder whether this absence and longing for gay male friendship and community is the final big hurdle to living a more fulfilled, connected, and liberated life.

Over time, my desire for gay male friendships was given a Band-Aid, manufactured through the normative cultural adage that I heard while growing up: simply surround yourself with "good people" in your life. Although I believe this adage captures a much-needed focus to forge interpersonal connections with "good people," I think it fails to highlight how important shared cultural identification can be.

Although I have a lot of good people in my life, I can easily add that I still feel a sense of loneliness or absence with having no gay men with whom I identify or look to for support, or who might help me to negotiate the challenges and celebrate the beauty of our shared identities.

Concerns and Adjustments of Being the Gay Friend

> It should come as no surprise that gay men's close and best friends are other gay men who tend to be like themselves.

Nardi, 1999, p. 106

In my experience, gay men have more often been sexual partners or acquaintances. Generally speaking, my life in Fort Collins has been one absent of minority cocultural friendships at large. Although I have a small network of ethnic minority and two lesbian friends in town, established local connections with other gay men are more clearly absent. In fact, among the many friends in my various networks of career, neighbors, and community, *I* am the one, almost exclusively, who happens to be gay.

Although outsiders often peg me as the token gay, U.S. ethnic minority in our groups, my own friends do not make me feel tokenized, as I understand quite clearly that it is mostly a product of demographics and availability. When I came out in my mid-twenties, over a decade ago, I took great pride in the fact that my strong interpersonal and social skills would serve me well. However frightened I might have been at the time, I still believe that those skills helped me through my first major wave of coming out. In the years since, my perception is that the lack of gay male friends has contributed to the challenges of achieving identification with other gay men and with those pieces of myself.

Perhaps over time and with demographic nonavailability, I have socialized myself to become accustomed to being the sole gay guy; perhaps my interactive distance from gay men and my negotiation within predominant, heterosexual communities has made for an inevitable, slow assimilation into the ever-present, dominant-majority culture. This identity distancing and settling may in fact help explain my sensitivity and frustration with being told that I am "straight acting." In my eyes, I am simply being me. When my gay male friends who live in other cities, like Seattle, San Francisco, Austin, Barcelona, Rio, and London, ask me about hanging out with other men in gay establishments or locally, I have little to report, since that is not the cultural scene available to me. In my community, I relax and socialize almost exclusively in cafes, pubs, and restaurants that are frequented predominantly by heterosexual individuals and families. Of course, the other side of the coin is that my gay friends interact very little with straight men. I often joke and tell them that the only heterosexual men they "know" are on television.

Recently, while sitting around having appetizers, drinks, and friendly conversation, I informally asked a couple of straight male friends what they thought it would be like without having other straight men to befriend. Most of them agreed that they could not conceive of *not* having their buddies around, and also agreed that if gay men, myself included, were their primary or only source of male friendship, they would likely feel a bit at a loss or in need of others who they believe would share their experiences and their perspectives. So, I emphasized quickly that, as a male friend who happens to be gay, I do not seem to provide holistic connection for them for reasons of cultural identification. They are clear that they like me a lot and believe I am a great guy who is a lot of fun. But to have only gay men as their primary or only source of friendship would not be enough for them.

When I told them that what they expressed is often how I feel, they began to understand. I think they have come to believe (with good reason) that the divisions of straight and gay do not make a difference with regard to our friendship, particularly because they identify as socially progressive, and likely because they have had the privilege of having access to both straight men and at least one gay man in their long-term friendship network. I also gathered that they thought being my friend, or simply being who they are *as* my friend, was enough for *me* to feel fulfilled, i.e., they provide everything a friend is supposed to. For all that we offer each other, I think we came to see that we could not provide the cultural identification that we can only get from befriending other men of our shared sexual orientation, or as Nardi (1999) calls it, "The Magic of Sympathy and Identification" (p. 102).

I know that even though our friendships with each other as one gay and many straight men are fun and connected, perhaps even historically progressive, I now realize how much I desire to have men in my daily life who share the experience of being out and gay. At the same time, while I have shared this concern with many people, in all honesty, there is a part of me that has become accustomed to being the sole gay Boi, so I have some reservations as to how well I would actually do being more a part of a gay community.

Most of my adult life has been about moving from context to context where negotiating the multiple-minority aspects of cultural identity, *the difference,* has been in some way pronounced. I have watched myself grow quite differently from my three siblings, who have always lived near our parents and who are more culturally collectivistic and in sync with the larger family ways of being. All of them seem to be more at ease when interacting with the multitude of diversity present in their daily lives. But, I know that there is part of me who has learned to survive well as the sole U.S. ethnic minority, sole working-class kid, and sole gay man in my many networks developed over the past nine years. So, over time, the bigger question for me has become: will moving to an area where there is more diversity presence bring about more peace of mind and heart, or will it disrupt too strongly my sense of cultural identity nurtured to this point as more often than not the lone minority, the sole gay male friend living *in situ*?

Imperatives for Enhancing Connections of Gay Male Friendships

> Numerous homosexual men—ranging in age from twenty-five to fifty and in style from swish to macho—have informed me that friendship is, indeed, absolutely critical to their lives.
>
> Miller, 1983, p. 136

Over the years, friends and family have asked me if my chosen life when accepting a career offer away from cosmopolitan cities was purposeful. At the beginning, it was, but mostly due to a need to sober up and slow my life down after experiencing relational loss (Aoki, 2003, 2004). In the back of my mind, I have always wondered about living more connected to a larger LGBTQ population. At the same time, living too centrally within a predominately gay life might equally unsettle me, no longer due to internalized homophobia, but rather to my own fear of getting caught up again in "the fast lane" and potential addiction. But, at age thirty-eight, my youthful mind and heart have learned to live better. In fact, lately I have been thinking more specifically about how I can maximize my skills and energies to help out my gay brothers who are aging and/or running the course of addictions.

Attention to these cultural problems for forging enhanced gay male friendships seems more critical then ever. Over the last few years, my own experiences provided me with a different picture of gay aging identity. Although I still travel and enjoy nightlife, beach time, and dancing, I have become somewhat more settled as an artist and a writer/professor. And although I have two wonderful men who I see with consistency, they both live in different cities, and we all continue to live on our own. As my heterosexual friends have become busier with their coupled, married, and child-filled lives, I can see that my life is different from what the sociocultural structure typically supports. And, if I am noticing these changes and concerns and in how, if at all, it fits into some culturally conceived structure, I imagine there are many older gay men who remain on their own and who are increasingly in need of the support and understanding that perhaps only other gay men might provide. Herein lies a humanistic imperative to understand better how and why we need to nurture our gay male friendships.

On the addiction front (my own was alcohol abuse), I have become more and more convinced that, as a gay man, I must step up and help others like me. As Ghaziani (2005) states: "Our vision should focus on fostering a healthy celebration rather than demonizing a sub-population of gay and bisexual men" (p. 23). For most of my life, I was raised and socialized to help others through the lessons learned from our own experiences. And despite my own lack of everyday connection to gay men, the gay scene, and to larger gay communities, I believe I have something to offer; I believe I have learned much about living well; and I believe I have turned my life around and sidestepped additional roadblocks by putting energy into my career, community service, art/writing, and, most important, my family relations and friendships, in whatever form they have taken.

The path of alcohol abuse was one of the darker periods of my life. It does not take much effort to remember how much I hated myself and how much I hated living as closeted and misguided. I wonder how differently things might have turned out had I been able to establish a connection earlier on with a healthy and positive-minded gay man. But no one I knew back then identified as such. For many years,

I have worked to offer support to my students, several of whom have struggled with coming out and with addiction. I often see the thankfulness in their eyes when some of them find the path to sobriety and integrity in working to become healthier and happier. Although not the typical friendship model, I have learned that friendship comes in many forms and requires a variety of caring practices and complex negotiations, particularly due to social stigmas that often influence the chain of inequities. In knowing that there are gay men out there struggling to develop better self-concepts and a healthier life course, it is clear that forging gay male friendships of *humanistic* substance is one possible deterrent to walking alone.

In this essay, I have explored personal life experiences within my everyday cultural context to assess the potential implications for the absence—and presence—of gay male friendships. As an individual who has limited daily connection to gay men, I wander through literature and human stories, more so than I actually know through my own experiences, and wonder what the challenges and benefits of living among a group of gay male friends might be like. But the concept of empowerment through a minority voice and perspective, and through friendships and allies is something I have come to know intimately when working to effect personal change. As Nardi (1999) offers:

> Friendship, perhaps in and of itself, may have the kinds of transforming power necessary to effect real, political changes. This may be even more the case for gay men's friendships, which challenge the social construction of heterosexual masculinity in the way it gets enacted, legitimated, and reproduced by gay people . . . Gay men's friendships might someday lead all men to a new, more modern, form of the heroic friendships of the past— one in which valor, bravery, and devotion are inextricably linked to intimacy, sharing, personal disclosure, vulnerability, and emotional support. (pp. 205-206)

As I think about the type of person my parents raised me to be, I know that the qualities and characteristics noted above are ones that I find foundational to declaring pride in the gay man that I have worked to become. My hope is that these qualities will also be ones that are identified in me by more gay men who, one day, will be proud to call me a friend.

NOTES

1. In his book, *"We Are Lincoln Men": Abraham Lincoln and His Friends,* Donald (2003), asserts: "Presently, I discovered that most ideas about friendship derive from philosophical analyses. It is easy to trace a line of intellectual descent from Emanuel Kant to Michel Montaigne to St. Thomas Aquinas to Cicero, all of whom wrote treatises on friendship. And, in turn, their ideas derive from the Nicomachean Ethics of Aristotle. Over the centuries, Aristotle's typology of friendship has remained fundamental. There are, Aristotle shows, three basic kinds of friendship . . . 'enjoyable' friendships . . . 'useful' friendships . . . and there are 'perfect' or 'complete' friendships" (p. xv).

2. The woman friend noted here is a self-avowed "fag hag." Of course, this term is disliked strongly by some individuals, but she claims to use both terms of the appellation in resistive and empowering ways. On the relationship between straight women and gay men, Malone (1980) states, "A gay man who is arriving at a more positive feeling about his homosexuality and a straight woman who is discovering a heightened sense of her own independence are traveling in the same direction, even if along different paths. Both, in essence, are reaching out toward an enhanced certainty of their own worth, and in many cases they are able to assist one another in taking new steps forward" (p. 5). I believe this relational description of friendship suits us well. Despite the absence of gay male friends, my "straight" woman friend has been a strong supporter. I believe that she has helped make my relations with straight men in the local community possible.

3. Nardi (1999) explores the intersection of friendship and sex. He states, "Probably the most common question gay men ask me when I tell them about my research is that of whether I'm going to talk about gay men's friendship and sex. To me this suggests that some powerful connections exist in their minds between gay friendships and gay sexual relationships . . . Without comparable data over time, it is difficult to show whether the incidence of sex between friends has increased, decreased, or stayed the same, let alone whether the change—if in fact there has been one—is related to any kind of incest taboo [the chosen 'family' metaphor]" (p. 75). In my own life, while I hold respectful and friendly relations with several gay men in the local or surrounding area, I do not see these men consistently, and when I do, sex is typically a part of the connection. Many of my closest friends question whether I should really use the term friend for men with whom I have had sexual relations. So the debate continues.

REFERENCES

Aoki, E. (2003). Making space in the classroom for my gay identity: A letter I've been wanting to write. In *Teaching diversity: Challenges and complexities, identities and integrity.* B. Timpson, S. Canetto, E. Borrayo, & R. Yang (Eds.) (pp. 91-102). Madison Wisconsin: Atwood Publishing.

Aoki, E. (2004). An interpersonal and intercultural embrace: A letter of reflection on my gay male relational connections. *Journal of Couple & Relationship Therapy, 3*(2/3), 111-121.

Donald, D. H. (2003). *"We are Lincoln men": Abraham Lincoln and his friends.* New York: Simon & Schuster.

Ghaziani, A. (2005). The circuit party's Faustian bargain. *The Gay & Lesbian Review Worldwide, 12*(4), 21-23.

Malone, J. (1980). *Straight women/gay men: A special relationship.* New York: The Dial Press.

Miller, S. (1983). *Men and friendship.* Boston: Houghton Mifflin Company.

Nardi, P. M. (1999). *Gay men's friendships: Invincible communities.* Chicago: University of Chicago Press.

Vernon, M. (2005). *The philosophy of friendship.* Houndmills, Basingstoke, Hampshire: Palgrave Macmillan.

– 15 –

Friends:
When Are They Necessary?

Jeffrey Dudgeon

As I start to write this essay on Christmas Eve, I have just buried my older cat Shadow in the back garden, pondering whether or not she was a friend. She was thirteen and had always been a disappointment. I rarely took much notice of her and she tended to avoid me except around the feeding bowl. However, if she went missing for any length of time, I would worry greatly and start searching the house, then the garden, and finally the street. That I think signifies she constituted a friend: a fixture you appreciate but rarely expect much of. In contrast, my other cat, Darcy, is a lover, who hangs around me all the time, like a heat-seeking missile. She is a user, not a friend.

Two days earlier, I found Shadow at the side of the house—cold, barely alive, and unable to move her legs, as if she had had a stroke. She died an hour later shortly before her terminal appointment with the vet.

On the Meaning of Friendship Between Gay Men

I am of that modern gay generation when having gay friends became a possibility. My initial teenage need, however, was to have any friend who appreciated me and who shared my mildly rebellious outlook. I had not been a gregarious child and thus lacked a peer group.

These friendships were only achieved with some effort. And I paid the price for falling in love with several of my new mates—and failing miserably—possibly as a consequence of not having had the courage to advise them of my feelings. Nor could I ask where gays were to be found, a question that could hardly have been framed let alone answered, even during the Cuban Missile Crisis when I expected to die. This was the case despite my friends' right-on, if underexperienced, attitudes toward matters such as homosexual law reform. These straight school chums, however, filled so many of my life spaces that I was able to function without sex or love or, more accurately, not driven into hopeless depression, until I was nineteen.

I recently found something I had written during that 1962 Cuban Crisis. This was a school exercise book, the only one I retained. In a remarkably brief homework essay entitled "Four Minutes to Go," I wrote:

> The ideal place to go would be in a small party in a small room with my twenty odd best friends and a record player turned up loud. The only thing I would be able to think of would be the happy times we had all had together. Myself or anyone else who wished to start relating personal intimacies of unfortunate events from the past could not because of the noise. I could only then think of myself, that it was now all over, everyone would go together, not just me and a few others more miserable. There would be no discrimination in the world for the first time ever . . . and then I would take my partner and we would twist ourselves out of this creation both, I know, thinking how unfair it was that Harold Wilson had not had a chance to become Prime Minister.

Obviously I felt at sixteen that I had more friends than I realized while, at the same time, recognizing that discrimination was a part of everyday life.

In Belfast, in the mid-1960s, when I did come out, I discovered gays did not do friends. Sex was a hard enough achievement since nobody had flats, cars were rare, and we were subject to the vagaries of the weather and our parents. I was living in a small city of half a million with a single gay bar, which shut down at 10 p.m. It had a clientele of perhaps fifty gay men—and two lesbians. This was apart from the "deaf and dumb" customers who filled the front half of the space in a miasma of silence, barring the noise of hands whizzing about.

With so few males to choose from, undesirable looks, a degree of straight-acting intellectuality, and the handicap of my young age, I was not only unlucky in the friendship department, I was not particularly blessed in the sexual one either. Most of the talent was literally on the point of departure, having a little courage to dabble locally just prior to fleeing to London, where the grass was reputedly greener and certainly more often cropped.

Perhaps my finest pickup involved driving in my mother's car way up the Antrim coast road with Adam, who lived in Larne, and backing into a lay-by only to have the rear wheels drop twelve inches down into a runnel. It took about an hour to build a platform to release the car, and there was only a moment left for a rushed hand job before I had to deliver Adam home. He left for a nursing course in England a few weeks later.

University days in the neighboring bigger, and for me foreign, city of Dublin saw the beginnings of gay friendships but they were based largely on student sisterhood or local gay coteries. My postgraduate migration to London lasted a year and proved only one thing: that the metropolis was not particularly attractive unless one was of the correct cultural persuasion or was preoccupied entirely by sex. Even the incipient gay liberation movement seemed to lack people of character.

Coming back to Belfast in 1973 after that failed migration I discovered the early stages of the gay liberation movement. It was based in the Queen's University of Belfast but had as many members from the town as it did from the University. Within a matter of days, I made a set of friends who have lasted over thirty years. That is not to say some did not become lovers and, if not, were seriously desired. What however happened overnight was that the pool of potential friends, that is gays who were attractive, admirable, and lovable, suddenly, for the first time, became available.

We were to be shaped in struggle as we took on the forces of local oppression in the early, indeed the worst, period of our civil war. It ran for over thirty years from 1969 leading eventually to 3,000 dead—the U.S. equivalent of half a million corpses or its own civil war. In 1972, the worst year, 500 people were killed. But we were greater than that war and felt angry and invincible, buoyed up by our masculinist solidarity. We even took over the nightlife of a deserted city where few dared leave their homes after darkness fell.

Belfast was a crazy, vicious place. The city center was surrounded by a ring of steel fencing with one or two entrances and exits manned by armed soldiers or police who had to search the gays, and a few transsexuals and drag artists, as we entered. Quite literally, the gay bar at the time, the Chariot Rooms, was about the only place open at night. Army duck patrols, as a consequence, were drawn in by the lights and the music. They then wended their way round the dance floor with some soldiers occasionally asking a mate to look after their rifle so as to be freer to join in the more energetic dances. Our own gay lib discos at the university, after the drinking students had headed home, became enormously popular, being again the only venue open late in that part of the city. A few straight (or not so straight) students would drift down to the newly named Mandela Hall, adding to the eclectic crew, which at the highest point, numbered over 300. Five years of being a doorman and bouncer who hates personal violence, nevertheless, earned me a few punches and kicks and few thanks.

In the end, our patchwork of loves and friendships prevailed, even when we became subject to a long series of searches, arrests, and impending charges for adult male sexual activity. Ironically this was when we were also beginning to influence our masters in London, who had taken political control of Northern Ireland in 1974, getting them to believe that decriminalization was a proper and appropriate policy. In that pre-human rights era, grudging concessions were the best we could hope for. Unfortunately the newly reformed police believed their job was now to behave like an English constabulary. And what did an English force do? Why round up the local queers, of course.

The 1976 gay raids tested us, if not to destruction, certainly to the point where we realized we could survive through solidarity and organization. It all started with one mother finding a letter from her son's boyfriend in his pocket before washing his clothes. She was well connected and foolishly complained to a high-up policeman. Her son had been staying in my house, having been dumped on us by that same boyfriend. As a kindness, he had donated a bag of grass to my housemate and the search warrant was to be made out in relation to the marijuana. I was then arrested along with my other housemate who was straight. Interrogated for five hours, I was released, but every piece of paper found in my house was held. It was eventually returned with red markings where the police felt they had incriminating evidence, such as a letter from my Canadian boyfriend, Douglas, then working in Ghana, telling me to check myself for crabs—which were not to be found.

As always, what started out as a single complaint became part of a program of raids involving all the committee members of the Northern Ireland Gay Rights Association (NIGRA) and its associate befriending group, Cara-Friend. This culminated in my being raided again. Several weeks later while staying with Douglas, we were woken up on a Saturday morning by a ring at the door. I looked out of the bedroom window to see my smirking interrogators below. We dressed at high speed. Douglas refused to open the door until he saw a search warrant. They threatened to break it down. He yielded but had time to ring a solicitor. Refusing to accompany them to the police station, he was arrested.

Ultimately, we and two others were sent for prosecution. Only the intervention of the Attorney General in London prevented such an absurdity. The consequences for several others were more significant: physical damage and impairment of job and academic prospects. Oddly the guy with the eighteen-year-old boyfriend and another whose teenage lover was the son of a top Protestant paramilitary were not picked out for prosecution, while we two, both over twenty-one, were to be sent forward. That son is now a well-known journalist and TV commentator in London. The other boy, unloved in Belfast because it turned out he had been coaxed to side with the police, fled to London and was never seen again. I often wonder if his mother regretted her actions. She certainly ensured that she lost her son.

Our friendships prospered then in protest and activity, which is what I am sure many others involved in the gay movement, in its broadest sense, will also have found. Michael Novotny and his friends in the American version of *Queer as Folk* still exhibit those tendencies even when forged in 1990s Pittsburgh.

Having said all this, it is harder to make friends as you get older. This is not a peculiarly gay thing but, if you do not have children and grandchildren, it is unlikely new people will come your way unless you are a constant devotee of gay bars or chat rooms. After your thirties, you quite simply no longer have the same opportunities or perhaps the personal flexibility to make new or more friends in any numbers. Perhaps F. Scott Fitzgerald was right when he said something like, "It is in our thirties that we want friends. In our forties, we know they won't save us any more than love did."

It was true in my case. The worst fear of a mother is that, as a gay man, you will end up alone, unwanted, and neglected. And I shared that terrible fear of future loneliness. Little did we know, despite those parental concerns—which partially prompted them to have children—that one's need for company diminishes over time and the notion of a quiet night on one's own becomes amazingly appealing. Not every night, but I can certainly take a run of three or four with equanimity.

A test of your friendship quotient is your Christmas card list. I find I rarely now add a new name, and more often delete a friend due to them succumbing to the scourges of alcoholism, breast cancer, or AIDS, though the last has been thankfully rare in provincial Belfast. This confirms again that the making of friends is a young person's thing. They just do not come your way after a certain age. One's older acquaintances have already been tested and rejected, and you would expect to need some sort of extraordinary corporeal magnet to draw in the younger gay man, especially as they do not do history or experience. Most anyway. Belfast has only very recently found itself attractive to economic migrants who gratifyingly want to hear the old stories. They are experientially in an equivalent of that 1970s period so I am able to talk through their questions and uncertainties and am called upon to provide conversation, the local youth having lost the art.

Old lovers also make good friends, particularly if you started out together having common pursuits and mutual interests. I am still Douglas's friend, even if he spends half the year in retirement in Prince Edward Island only returning to Belfast to escape its harsh winter. You should also have common experiences as they enable people to maintain connections in friendship.

Without friends, surely you will atrophy. But I've found that, later in life, even though their number lessens, you need not feel diminished by their lack.

Notes from the Apocalypse:
A Week with Katrina

Marc E. Vargo

It was August 27, 2005, and I was looking forward to a quiet weekend at home in the French Quarter. My partner Michael had rented a British comedy that had just come out on DVD, and I was planning to begin writing a biography of Hans Christian Andersen. And that's what I'd started doing on that muggy Saturday morning when Michael called from the hotel where he worked, his voice filled with concern.

"Have you seen TV today?" he asked.

"No," I replied. "Why?"

"They're saying there's a hurricane headed our way. Take a look at the Weather Channel. I'll call you back in a minute," he said.

Slightly frustrated by the interruption, I put aside my work and trudged downstairs to check the weather report. That's when I discovered that he was right; it didn't look good for us. A category-three hurricane was headed in our direction, although it was still a couple of days away. I decided not to worry, though. Having lived on the Gulf Coast for many years, I knew that hurricanes were notoriously unpredictable, often veering at the last minute and losing strength before making landfall. Evacuation was seldom necessary. So, on the assumption that this was yet another false alarm, I went back to work on the life story of Andersen. When Michael called again a few minutes later, I told him I didn't think the storm was worth worrying about and saw no reason for us to leave. Evidently, thousands of other New Orleanians felt the same way.

On the Meaning of Friendship Between Gay Men

Later that morning, I went to my health club where a dozen men clad in towels gathered around a television and watched the weather updates. Although a handful looked apprehensive, most dismissed the warnings as exaggerated and said they had no plans to leave the city. One young newcomer made it a point to scoff at the long-held notion that a major hurricane would trigger widespread flooding in New Orleans, insisting it was an impossibility. Little did we know.

Sunday, August 28th

The next morning, everything changed. When I awoke, I learned that Katrina had turned into a category-five storm, the most intense grade, and was headed dead-on toward New Orleans. It also had Gulfport in its sights, the home of my seventy-six-year-old mother. When I called her, I found that she was refusing to evacuate because the highways were in gridlock, a state of affairs posing the horrific possibility of drowning in one's car when the storm struck. Given this harrowing prospect, she had decided to stay put and take her chances. Besides, she didn't want to leave behind her two dogs, neither of whom did well with lengthy car trips.

Michael and I decided to make a run for it, however; a superstorm was not to be taken lightly. At once, we set to work preparing our three cats for a trip to Kentwood, a village two hours northwest of New Orleans where Michael's parents operate a horse farm. (Kentwood is also the hometown of Britney Spears, an absurd piece of trivia that leapt into my mind.) His family had evacuated to Oklahoma, so the farm was unoccupied.

Fate, however, had other plans for us. We soon discovered that we couldn't leave the French Quarter because the parking garage where we kept our car had been padlocked, meaning that scores of vehicles, including our own, were trapped inside it. Although we were in the path of a killer cyclone, a lapse in judgment by a parking garage manager prevented us from escaping.

Desperate, I called the police and asked that they help us release our car, but was told they were not authorized to do this, that the facility was private property. Naturally, this was not news I wanted to hear.

"We're screwed," I told Michael.

"It'll be alright," he reassured me. "We'll ride out the storm. But remind me to sue the fools at the garage if we get through this."

Monday, August 29th

The following morning, the hurricane hit with savage fury, the wind screaming as it ravaged the city. Early on, it downed a large magnolia tree in our courtyard, while littering our property with a bizarre hodgepodge of objects, from a martini shaker to a fishing pole. It also hurled part of our roof to the ground, the shingles shattering like glass. We were safe inside, though, with the stately brick townhouse, which had been built two decades before the Civil War, braving the storm. Only later would we learn that it had suffered structural damage and would need to be dismantled and rebuilt.

Finally, several hours later, the winds died down as Katrina continued her northward assault toward Gulfport and my mother. But for Michael and me, the worst was over, or so it seemed, and we went outside to survey the damage.

All in all, the French Quarter had withstood the onslaught remarkably well, a fact that raised our spirits. Glad it was over, we began cleaning up the courtyard, our assumption being that we would get on with our lives. Again, little did we know.

Tuesday, August 30th

Twenty-four hours later, the power was still off and the heat was sickening. Since there was nothing else to do, we ventured onto the street, where we noticed a pool of water in front of our house and figured it was the result of a ruptured water main. We also noticed there were no cops in sight, a peculiar absence given the circumstances. We assumed that something dire must be happening elsewhere in the city, with our speculation being confirmed a few minutes later when my brother called from Illinois to tell us about a new CNN report: New Orleans' business district had been devastated, including the Hyatt Regency, and rescue operations were underway.

Curious, Michael and I walked to the ill-starred hotel, where we were stunned to find that one of its wings had been blown out. The image was surreal, a scene from Sarajevo. We were equally startled to find floodwaters surrounding the hotel and the Superdome adjacent to it, along with National Guardsmen maneuvering around both structures in boats. It was then that a soldier told us that the levees were crumbling and New Orleans was going under. Suddenly we understood that the water in front of our house had not been caused by a damaged water main. The truth was far more terrible.

By the time we returned home, the water had risen dramatically. It was two-feet deep in our section of the Quarter, although most of the historic district remained dry. Even more distressing, looting had broken out, with a mob shattering the windows of a dress shop popular with trannies. Police fired shots into the air to scare off the thieves. This was two blocks from our house and occurred in the middle of the day.

"We've got to get the hell out of here," I said.

"Let's check the garage again," Michael replied.

As before, it was locked. But this time we noticed that the manager had taped a note to one of the exit doors, a soaked message with a phone number for customers to call. When we did, we found it was a wrong number. It was a woman's cell phone and she had no idea why she kept receiving urgent pleas from people trying to escape from the drowning city.

"We'll add that piece of information to the lawsuit," Michael said.

Minutes later, the situation worsened, with looters raiding a grocery store in our neighborhood. On the sidewalks, people were also snatching one another's spoils, the robberies persisting after leaving the store. Gangs of men pushed the store's freezers down the streets of the Quarter, only to be met by Humvees loaded with armed Guardsmen. One looter glared at Michael with a rabid look in his eyes and came toward us in the water, but stopped as we approached a cluster of employees near the Royal Sonesta Hotel on Bourbon Street where Michael worked. It was then that we decided to seek refuge at the hotel. Staying at home was far too risky because of the mayhem in the streets and fleeing the city remained an impossibility because our car was locked away. Then, too, the evacuation routes were still impassable. Amplifying the hopelessness of the situation, a panicked policeman told me—speciously, it turned out—that a twenty-two-foot wall of water was coming our way and would not stop until it reached the Gulf of Mexico.

The only positive note was the Royal Sonesta Hotel itself, which offered us free room and board for as long as we needed it and whose remaining staff was the epitome of benevolence. Although the hotel had no water or electricity, we felt safer in a building surrounded by National Guardsmen, police officers, and private guards. At the same time, it was not unlike the film *Hotel Rwanda* in that we were trapped inside a hotel encompassed by anarchy.

It was during that night, for instance, that all manner of violence erupted within blocks of the hotel—in the Superdome, at the Convention Center, and on the city streets. In our room in the sweltering August night, we could hear the thrashing of helicopter blades and the wailing of police sirens hour after hour. For me, it proved to be another sleepless night, although Michael and the cats, exhausted, let loose with a chorus of snores. It was at this point that I realized this might well be the last night of our lives, a searing insight that caused me to become even more determined to find an evacuation route the next morning. As it happened, an hour or so later I heard a bus pull up outside the hotel, a bus that had to have come from outside of the city.

Wednesday, August 31st

At daybreak, I found that I was right. The sole remaining desk clerk told me that the hotel's manager had arranged for a bus to enter New Orleans the evening before, its mission being to take a group of stranded French tourists to the Houston airport. This meant, then, that an escape route had indeed opened up. Seizing the opportunity, Michael obtained the details of the route from a nearby policeman, while I gained permission to cut off the lock at the parking garage and free our car. Moving now at hyperspeed, we were soon on the road.

Driving past the Convention Center, we saw scores of disaster victims camped outside in the heat and stench. Crossing the Crescent City Connection, the three-mile bridge that stretches across the Mississippi River, we also saw refugees plodding toward the other side, their belongings on their backs or in grocery carts. Only later would we learn that these unfortunates had been met by shotgun-wielding men with guard dogs on the other side of the bridge. Rather than help the evacuees escape the perils of the city, authorities in the drab suburban town of Gretna forced them to walk back to New Orleans in spite of the city's rising waters, food shortages, and escalating brutality. For the most part, these were white people who did not want black people in their town. As for the refugees, they included children, women, and the elderly.

Thursday, September 1st

Michael and I spent the ensuing days on his family's vacant horse farm. At the house in which we were staying, part of the roof had blown off, the carport had collapsed, and insulation littered the yard. There was no electricity or running water, and the Louisiana sun caused the temperature to hover in the high nineties. For the next three days, this was our home and we were glad to have it. At least our lives were not in jeopardy here, just our health. And this became apparent before long, with the onset of headaches and dizziness.

Finally, during what would prove to be our last day in Kentwood, I recalled something important: I had an acquaintance, Mark Pang, who lived in Jackson, Mississippi, a city two hours north of us. A couple of years earlier, Mark had been a resident of New Orleans, where he and I had worked together at the same agency. I had always liked him and especially appreciated the fact that, for the Deep South, he was a rare breed—a Hawaii-born, gay psychologist. Now, hoping he might still be residing in Jackson, I spent the next hour trying to get through to directory assistance to track down his number. When at last I reached his home phone, a man answered, explained that Mark wasn't there at the moment, and asked if I wanted to leave a message. When I told him my name and began explaining my circumstances, he interrupted me.

"Marc Vargo?" he blurted out. "This is Steve! Steve Gentile. Are you okay?"

Steve was another gay psychologist from New Orleans, and, like Mark Pang, had worked at the same agency with me. It turned out that Steve and his partner Tim had taken refuge at Mark's place in Jackson shortly before the hurricane made landfall on the Louisiana coast. "Get up here!" Steve insisted when he found out that Michael and I were living in desolate conditions. "It'll be fine with Mark," he assured me. A few minutes later, Tim got on the line and urged us to come as well. And so we went in search of gasoline, a rare commodity at the moment, which we found in a shed.

As we were preparing for the drive north, the phone rang. It was my brother and he was elated. My mother had just called from a Red Cross shelter to tell him she was alive and to find out about Michael and me. She and her pets had made it through the storm and the tidal surge and were preparing to return home, albeit to a house with a gaping hole in the roof. All the same, she, like us, rejoiced in the fact that everyone in our families had survived. Today had been a wonderful day, all things considered.

Saturday, September 3rd

When Michael and I, along with our trio of cats, arrived at Mark's address in Jackson the following day, we were pleasantly surprised by the house itself. A gracious Southern home nestled in the Old Towne section of Mississippi's capital city, it boasted oak trees and a swimming pool. Even better, it had electricity and running water.

At the door, we were met with handshakes and hugs by a good-humored guy by the name of John, yet another gay expatriate from the Big Easy. He showed us around the rambling house, then took us to our bedroom. It was a light, airy room with an adjoining bath, and he had placed cinnamon kisses on our pillows. A few days later, after he had boarded a flight to Texas, we learned that this had been John's bedroom during his impromptu stay and he had given it up so we could enjoy it after our dreadful days in the city and on the horse farm. We were touched by his generosity.

During the days that followed, Mark and the others were thoughtful as well. They didn't put us on display when we arrived, nor did they drill us about our hardships during Katrina and afterward. Instead, they allowed us to talk about these matters at our own pace. They also made sure we ate and drank well. And together we all stayed abreast of what remained of New Orleans' gay community, a community of which we had each been a part and would remain so, at least in spirit, wherever we might end up.

Among other things, we learned that on Labor Day weekend, the date of the gay community's annual Southern Decadence celebration, a handful of gay men and lesbians who had stayed behind staged a spur-of-the-moment parade in the French Quarter. Leading the procession was a bare-chested guy who carried a banner asking the question on everyone's mind: "Life Goes On?" As it stood, the fact that gay men and women were the first segment of the citizenry to host a parade after the catastrophe ensured that gay life in New Orleans would indeed go on.

As for Michael and me, the hospitality of Mark, Steve, Tim, and John illustrated to us, once again, the meaning of gay friendship, and particularly the importance of such bonds in the wake of a natural disaster. After facing the terrible power of Hurricane Katrina, the resultant anarchy of a city under siege, and the emotional isolation of a deserted horse farm, the arrival of a group of gay friends into our ruptured lives furnished us with a reassuring sense of comfort and connection. It was at this time that we began to feel that perhaps our world had not been totally devastated, that things might turn out alright after all. For us, then, the antidote to Katrina's fury and the urban nightmare that ensued was the embrace of a household of gay men, a perfect human presence that placed the two of us on the path to renewal.

– 17 –

Subject: friendship

Dan Martin and Michael Biello

Date: Sunday, November 20, 2005, 8:20am
From: Dan Martin <dan@biellomartin.com>
To: Michael Biello <michael@biellomartin.com>
Subject: friendship

Michael dear, I have an idea for how to make this friendship project happen. I thought maybe we could write e-mails back and forth. Even though we live and work together and our computers are located only twenty feet apart, it could be a way for us to create a focused exchange to consider what friendship is to me, you, us.

Let me know what you think.

Date: Tuesday, November 22, 2005, 2:11pm
From: Michael Biello <michael@biellomartin.com>
To: Dan Martin <dan@biellomartin.com>
Subject: friendship

On the Meaning of Friendship Between Gay Men

hi, loverfriend. i find your idea intriguing. let's give it a go.

dear old webster's definition of friend:

1. a person whom one knows well and is fond of—intimate associate—close acquaintance
2. a person on the same side in a struggle—one who is not an enemy or foe—ally
3. a supporter or sympathizer
4. something thought of as like a friend in being helpful—reliable, etc.
5. a member of the society of friends—quaker

my definition of a friend is you.
there is all the beauty and unbeauty
present even when you run in the opposite direction,
a part of who I am,
my chosen family,
my brother,
my lover.

for me friendship goes a bit beyond webster,
friends even when we disagree.
friendship is deeper than what we see on the surface,
deeper than what we believe makes a friend.
friendship is deeper than ourselves,
based on trust
respect
honor
acceptance
love
truth.
being the human beings that we are, sometimes these qualities collapse.
friendship heals itself if it is true friendship.

you are my friend because you are in my life in a real way.
surface is not an option.
are there different levels of friendship?
if so, ours is the level of friendship I like living in—deep.

Date: Friday, November 25, 2005, 9:42am
From: Dan Martin <dan@biellomartin.com>
To: Michael Biello <michael@biellomartin.com>
Subject: friendship

Michael, Thanks for your e-mail and for your (usual) wonderful poetry of words. Focused and playful and romantic. Some feel like lyrics, but I will hold off setting them to music since we are trying to write a chapter and not a song!

I like your description of our friendship as "deep." I wonder if it feels this way because of all the other aspects of relationship that we share and perhaps the friendship part underlies everything else—like a foundation or a root. Or maybe the deepness of our friendship was instant and became the reason we were able to build so much upon it.

I remember when I first met you—thirty-plus years ago. My journal entry was something like: "I've been spending time with a new person, Michael, who's being very nice to me, taking time to listen." As simple and powerful as that!

I think about the complexity of our relationship, and how we share so many dimensions of life together:

love
family
history
creativity
business
roommates.

How could I begin to isolate and describe the part that is friendship?

Perhaps friendship is the least possessive and opinionated of all these. The part that says, "Yes, go off and do that." "This will be best for you." "Yes, I'll make time to talk with you now even though I was headed somewhere else." Giving priority to each other's well-being even when it conflicts with the other desires or choices like finances, eroticism, or...

If I were to improvise at the piano on the theme of friendship, I wonder what it would sound like? Maybe a simple counterpoint of melody and harmony played with easy movement between the left and right hands. Separate movement of the hands but with a steady support throughout shifting minor and major themes. Or maybe it should be more basic: a repeated tone in the mid/low range, a steady pulse.

Date: Saturday, December 3, 2005, 9:03am
From: Michael Biello <michael@biellomartin.com>
To: Dan Martin <dan@biellomartin.com>
Subject: friendship

the creative part of our relationship comes through as i read your words. it makes me think that maybe creativity is the key to a true friendship. opening ourselves up beyond what we think friendship is, beyond what webster tells us, creating our own definition, our own red, green, and amber lights.

we do it with art and music, why not with friendship?

explore—edit—dissolve—create—re-create—color—black and white discover—dream—transform—inspire

if we invite creativity into our friendship, we can stay open to ourselves and one another forever changing—evolving—deepening.

totally feeling the friendship piece of our relationship these past few weeks. it's that crazy time of year again—the holiday frenzy in the gallery, family, friends, parties, dinners.

this puts pressure on our day-to-day experience, on our flow, so to speak.
somehow we do move through it—i believe friendship has everything to do with this flow.

these past few weeks our communication has been working wonders. it's not solving all of our "problems," but it does give me a place to rest my brain and get a new perspective.
you've been sharing yourself and this is good for me, not always what i want to hear, but i am listening and trying my best to learn some-

thing new about you each time. some of it I've heard before but hearing it again reminds me how special you are to me and, most important, how vital our friendship is. it all returns to that feeling of trust. i trust you.

even when we are way off balance, i know that somewhere deeper than our own selves we love one another and this love eventually comes to the frontline.

i am grateful to have you as my friend.

Date: Wednesday, December 7, 2005, 10:16am
From: Michael Biello <michael@biellomartin.com>
To: Dan Martin <dan@biellomartin.com>
Subject: friendship

dan, thanks for your patience yesterday. the holiday darkness and all else that comes with winter's time has a hold on me. your friendship helps me through, reminds me of it's temporary nature.
just visiting, feeling a bit clearer today. thanks.

i want to continue to dream and discover and open myself to the possibility of learning something new, finding new parts of myself that come with age, pieces that were not available before fifty. i feel it's time to explore what they might be for me and for us as a couple. change is always something we help guide each other through. change is in the air. we are doing well.

this, I believe, is part of being a good friend and lover.

friendship and love can be both active and passive. rises and rests; rests and rises. the key is to trust that it is always there even when it seems to disappear, at least that's how I feel with you. i guess that's what makes it true friendship. true love

Date: Friday, December 30, 2005, 10:36am
From: Dan Martin <dan@biellomartin.com>
To: Michael Biello <michael@biellomartin.com>
Subject: friendship

Michael dear, Apologies for all the time that has gone by since your last note. Yes, the holidays have done a number on me once again. I actually feel I'm handling them better than ever before, but still it feels like a long trudge up a high foggy hill. An endurance test. Trying my best to keep up with all my commitments—composing, notating, recording, the application deadlines, the new apartment renovations, all the social events, families—and surrounding everything is this weird feeling of pressure and melancholy that always seems to accompany the holidays—with odd and mysterious connections to past and future, dead relatives, children, and then throw in some bizarre consumer madness!

So, focusing on the subject at hand, at the present moment, I need to admit that I'm feeling a bit shaky and somewhat protective, especially as I feel what I perceive to be the hard edge of your impatience with me surfacing this morning. I guess I would ask, as a friend, that you try to keep being loving with me and keep allowing me the time and space to be myself in all my beauty and imperfection and potential—even at fifty-three!

And as I write these words I feel some of my own power and confidence flooding back and I see the flip side of this, recognizing my own judgments and wanting to heed my own call to be loving and open to all that you are.

I am in gratitude that you are a friend whom I can be honest with, writing and speaking my truth and trusting you will be able to hear it and that you will respond with your truth that I will be able to accept.

I don't know or can no longer tell what the difference between friendship and love is. I know that I have both with you.

Date: Friday, December 30, 2005, 11:41am
From: Michael Biello <michael@biellomartin.com>
To: Dan Martin <dan@biellomartin.com>
Subject: friendship

and i with you.